As One
Without
Authority

Also from Chalice Press
by Fred B. Craddock:

Craddock Stories
edited by Mike Graves and Richard F. Ward

As One Without Authority

Revised and with
New Sermons

FRED B. CRADDOCK

Chalice Press
St. Louis, Missouri

Cover design: Becky Hansen
Interior design: Wynn Younker
Art direction: Elizabeth Wright

This book is printed on acid-free, recycled paper.

Visit Chalice Press on the World Wide Web at
www.chalicepress.com

10 9 8 7 6 5 4 3 2 1   01 02 03

Library of Congress Cataloging–in–Publication Data

Craddock, Fred B.
   As one without authority / Fred B. Craddock. —4th ed.
     p.   cm.
   Includes bibliographical references.
   ISBN 0-8272-0026-9
   1. Preaching. I. Title.
BV4211.3 C73   2001
251— dc21   00-012058

Contents

Preface

When Jon L. Berquist, Academic Editor of Chalice Press, first approached me about re-issuing *As One Without Authority*, I hope he heard gratitude in my voice. I am grateful and honored that he sees in this book continuing value. What I know he heard in my voice was hesitation, or more correctly, hesitations.

When do you wish to undertake this project? As soon as possible. "As soon as possible" is an editor's expression for "yesterday." And what do I have to do to facilitate this re-issue? With several other deadlines waking me every morning, the question was crucial. I was quietly hoping Jon would say, "Nothing; grant us permission and we will reprint it," but both of us knew that was not going to happen. Obviously he had read the book and knew as well as I that the language in this 1969–1970 volume was not gender sensitive and was, therefore, offensive. Before I could even raise the issue, Jon was ahead of me: "We have editors who will repair the language."

What, then, are you asking of me? Three things. First, make any changes in the text that you wish. I nixed that request immediately. Were I to approach the book thinking, I should have said this, I should not have said that, I should be clearer here, I should update there, the result would not be this book but another one. So, I stood with Pilate: "What I have written I have written." Second, add three sermons to the Appendixes. I can do that. However, the one sermon already in the book was written for the book; the three I would add would be transcribed from tapes made at Cherry Log Christian Church and, therefore, would be congregation specific and oral in style. The differences will be obvious. Is that acceptable? Yes; send the tapes. (I confess to nervousness about this; oral and written styles are quite different.)

Third, and finally, write a brief Preface. Sure, I can do that; prefaces are usually personal and reflective and I am comfortable with such writing. However, I reminded Jon that often prefaces are written by others, usually friends or colleagues of authors. I know, he said, but we want you to write it. No problem.

I consented too easily, too soon. To write the Preface meant I had to again read the book; the task was unavoidable. I screwed up my courage to the sticking point and began—with the Endnotes. It seemed wise to recall those who were my conversation partners at the time of writing. This recollection would lead to a reconstruction in my mind of the atmosphere, the issues, the state of the church and its pulpit, the questions being asked by preachers and listeners, and the significant voices of the time. Anticipating some pain if not embarrassment, playing again an old tape, I was surprised and actually invigorated by the conversations of thirty years ago. To be sure, in those Endnotes were some museum names to a new generation of preachers, but to any generation of preachers, I would make three responses. One, the pulpit must be in conversation with the issues of its own time and the voices that address those issues. Two, the pulpit should engage the most thoughtful and substantive minds of its generation regardless of the views of those minds on matters vital to preaching. No one is well served if the preacher listens only to friendly voices and forages through books and journals only in search of an illustration. Three, a serious conversation about preaching has value beyond its own time. Important places in the mind need not only to be visited but revisited.

After lingering and remembering among the Endnotes, I moved to the text and read it again. Would it be vain to say I read what I had written with interest and profit? Vain or not, it is true.

So now I offer it to you as it was, and is.

Fred B. Craddock
Cherry Log, Georgia
January 2001

PART I

The Present Situation

Chapter 1

The Pulpit in the Shadows

We are all aware that in countless courts of opinion the verdict on preaching has been rendered and the sentence passed. All this slim volume asks is a stay of execution until one other witness be heard. The tardiness of this witness is not to be construed as dramatic timing. It is, rather, due to a cowardice born of that familiar fear of rising to defend that which has been derided by close and learned friends. And, in addition, one is painfully hesitant to speak in behalf of a defendant who is not entirely innocent of the charges brought against him.

The alarm felt by those of us still concerned about preaching is not a response solely to the noise outside in the street, where public disfavor and ridicule have been heaped upon the pulpit. On the contrary, most preachers are quite skilled at translating such criticism into "crosses to be borne" and appropriating for themselves the blessing lodged in some proper text, such as, "Beware when all men speak well of you." These are not new sounds; to a large extent, the pulpit has from the first century received poor reviews (2 Cor. 10:9–10). To explain this general reaction, perhaps one need not look for reasons profound; it may be simply that these critics have heard us preach!

More disturbing has been the nature and character of those who have been witnesses for the prosecution. Increasingly, the brows that frown upon the pulpit are not only intelligent, but often

3

theologically informed, and quite often deeply concerned about the Christian mission. Their judgments about preaching cannot be regarded as reflections of a general disinterest in religion, nor dismissed as the usual criticisms hurled at the familiar caricature in the pulpit, droning away in stained-glass tones with pretended convictions about matters uninteresting, unimportant, and untrue. Some of these critics have themselves been preachers in the churches. In short, the major cause for alarm is not the broadside from the public, nor the sniping from classroom sharpshooters, but the increasing number who are going AWOL from the pulpit. Some of these people move into forms of the ministry that carry no expectation of a sermon, or out of the ministry altogether. In addition, there are countless others who continue to preach, not because they regard it as an effective instrument of the church but because of the combined force of professional momentum and congregational demand.

It is the sober opinion of many concerned Christians, some who give the sermon and some who hear it, that preaching is an anachronism. It would be granted, of course, by all these critics that the pulpit has, in other generations, forcefully and effectively witnessed to the gospel, initiating personal and social change. It would be regarded by them as proper, therefore, for the church to celebrate the memory of preaching in ways appropriate to her gratitude and to affix plaques on old pulpits as an aid to those who tour the churches. But the church cannot live on the thin diet of fond memories. New forms of ministry are being forged and shaped overnight to meet the morning's need. And these ministries are without pulpit.

One need only look into the seminaries to get a clear picture of the tenuous position of preaching. Some seminaries offer little, or at best only marginal, work in homiletics. It should be said immediately, however, in defense of such lacunae, that there is, in some quarters, a serious reexamination of the wisdom of having instruction in preaching as a separate curriculum item. This reappraisal is due in part to an appreciation for the complexity of preaching and its inextricable relation to the other disciplines. It is in this mood that Joseph Sittler has written:

> And, therefore, the expectation must not be cherished that, save for modest and obvious instruction about voice, pace, organization, and such matters, preaching as a lively art of the church can be taught at all...Disciplines correlative

to preaching can be taught, but preaching as an act of witness cannot be taught.[1]

All too frequently, however, seminary education in preaching consists of training under a speech teacher or exposure to the toothless reminiscences of a kindly old pastor reactivated from retirement. In the former case, preaching is quite aside from the rest of the seminary curriculum because preaching so taught has its form defined not by the content of the gospel nor the nature of Christian faith but by Greek rhetoric. As will be discussed later, the separation of form and content is fatal for preaching, for it fails to recognize the theology implicit in the method of communication. When a person preaches, the method of communication, the movement of the sermon, reflects the hermeneutical principles, the view of the authority of scripture, church, and clergy, and especially one's doctrine of humanity. This is revealed verbally and nonverbally in the point of contact made with the listeners and the freedom to respond permitted them. It is a fact that much preaching contradicts by its method the content of its message. It is not reasonable to expect a speech teacher to guide a seminarian in a method of preaching that incarnates the message. The discussion of such a method is the major burden of this book. And, of course, when preaching is taught by a pastor, retired or active, the course suffers, deservedly or not, from that particular brand of harsh laughter reserved by students and faculty for that which lacks academic respectability. As a natural consequence, preaching continues for another generation as "a marginal annoyance on the record of a scientific age."[2]

This characterization of the minor role of preaching in some seminaries is not intended as an accusation of the seminaries as the source and cause of a poor pulpit. Seminaries not only create but reflect the general condition of the churches they serve and the cultures in which they live. It is in this larger context that the major reasons for the disrepute into which preaching has fallen are to be found. A brief examination of some of these reasons may function as the diagnosis that leads to recovery of health and power.

It is generally recognized that many blows struck against the pulpit come not because of its peculiar faults but because it is a part of a traditional and entrenched institution, and all such institutions—religious, political, or otherwise—are being called into question. Strong winds of change blow over the land, and strange new shadows fall across the comfortable hearths where we have taken long naps. Some pulpits feel threatened as the novelty of the new obscures distinctions between apparent and real values. Reactionary idealism, as the cutting edge of change, necessarily makes large room for error, but in the midst of uncertainty, it must not be overlooked that many pulpits have welcomed the interruption of triviality and are grateful for the chance to be faithful in such a time.

A primary reason, both in point of time and significance, for the general low estimate of preaching is to be found in the nature of American Christianity. Perhaps the most characteristic mark of the American church as distinguished from the church elsewhere in the world has been activism. The Social Gospel Movement was native to this soil and to the understanding of the Christian faith that is captured in the motto "Deeds, not words." After the churches in Europe have heatedly debated the truth claims of a theological position, the American churches appropriate that portion of it that will "work." In critical times, the demand for relevance becomes so strong that the sole canon by which a ministry is measured is the degree of its participation in the skirmish of the day. When this atmosphere prevails, the whole Bible is reduced to Matt. 25:31–46, and criticisms against preachers as those who "just talk" create a reaction of silent busyness. While this accent has been not only the power of the American church but its fundamental witness to the church elsewhere, it has at the same time unfairly obscured the place of the sermon. In fact, the power of the sermon to initiate and sustain movements for social change has often been overlooked because sermons were "words, words, words." While some American pulpits have been outstanding, on the average corner on an average Sunday, preaching has been tolerated and the ministers have given sermons that were tolerable. Where the expectation is low, the fulfillment is usually lower.

Implicit in what has just been said is the minimization of the power of words to effect anything: to create or to destroy, to bind or to loose, to bless or to curse. This common denial of the efficacy of words has been with us long enough to be enshrined in a number of proverbs: "Talk is cheap"; "It is not what you say but what you do that counts"; "I'd rather see a sermon than hear one any day"; "Sticks and stones may break my bones, but words…" Obviously, there is enough truth in these expressions to keep them alive. In them is some deserved judgment against a church that gives recitations, lifeless words cut off from the hearts and minds of those who speak and those who listen. Søren Kierkegaard, the great

Danish philosopher, captured this state of affairs in his parable of the man who saw in a shop window a sign, *Pants Pressed Here*. He went in and immediately began removing his pants. The startled shopkeeper stopped him, explaining that he did not press pants; he painted signs. Beneath these deprecatory statements about words lies a view of speaking that, if subscribed to, is fatal for preaching. Certainly no one can preach who has no respect for words, who allows them to creep over the tongue and sneak out the corners of the mouth, self-conscious and sheepish, as though hoping to fall to the ground and steal away unheard.

That there is in our time a language crisis, a general experience of the loss of the power of words, is all too evident. Needless to say, this means a crisis in preaching. The starting point for the study of homiletics has been radically shifted. All considerations of structure, unity, movement, use of text, and so forth, must wait upon the prior consideration of what words are and what they do. Any young preacher who does not take time to develop some grasp of the nature and meaning of words and of what happens when words are shared in communication will soon fall silent, frustrated, disenchanted, weary of the sound of her own voice, and convinced that what descended upon her was not a dove but an albatross. In these primary considerations, the preacher will find many resources, for the study of the meaning of words is a central issue in contemporary philosophy, theology, and biblical interpretation. This fact alone indicates the immensity of the problem, but it also holds rich prospects for the renewal of preaching.

Why in our time is a person "the victim of linguistic estrangement from his tradition and linguistic confusion among his contemporaries"?[3] Why the sickness of language, the degeneration of the streets and avenues of communication into "slum districts"?[4] Some partial answers lie near at hand.

No doubt the fact that we are today bombarded with words has contributed to the decay of meaning. By limitless new forms, made possible primarily by electronic media, we are surrounded by words. The eyes and ears have no relief, and all the old silent haunts are now scarred with billboards and invaded by public-address systems.

> When language is no longer related to silence, it loses its source of refreshment and renewal and therefore something of its substance…By taking it away from silence we have made language an orphan.[5]

A second reason for the loss of power and meaning in words may lie in the nature of traditional religious language. Gerhard Ebeling has properly observed that "out of mistrust of religious words there grows contempt for words as such."[6] But why this mistrust of religious language? It is in part, of course, due to the language lag that has always plagued the church, a hesitation to lay aside old terms and phrases for fear of laying aside something vital to the faith itself. Hence, unfortunately, the church has no retirement program for old words that fought well at Nicea, Chalcedon, and Augsburg; they are kept in the line of march even if the whole mission is slowed to a snail's pace and observers on the side are bent double in laughter.

In our time, however, the failure of the church's language has been accelerated by the ascendancy of the language of science. By this is meant not simply the vocabulary of science but the fundamental understanding of what words are and what they can and cannot do.

> Undoubtedly the modern revolution in the natural sciences has had a profound effect upon language—or better, upon our consciousness and conceptualization of language. Science has made us profoundly uneasy about how we can or cannot use language. It has brought on a new thirst for clarity, precision, and freedom from ambiguity, all to be construed in terms of the models of the scientific method itself.[7]

One's immediate response is favorable if this means simply that the church must do her homework, choose carefully her words, and be clear in her proclamation. But more than this is meant, for the model of the scientific method understands words as signs, as indicators pointing to information that can be verified. For language to be meaningful, it is said, it must keep itself to this task. Were the pulpit to acquiesce and promise to speak according to these rules, it would have to forfeit its evocative use of words, its use of language to create new situations, its use of the parable and the myth. Under such editorship, the church's language would be "cleaned up," striking all symbolic and mythological uses as preliterate, primitive, and meaningless. The results would, of course, be tragic. While the scientific use of language to designate is an important function of words and necessary to some disciplines, to permit words only this function would be sterilizing reductionism. Words have too many other rich and full functions in all human thinking, learning, feeling, and sharing to be pulled through this small knothole.

It is a tragic fact, however, that the pulpit in many places accepted this restricted and restricting view of language. Perhaps these preachers at first felt secure in the scientific world because it reinforced their view of their task: to communicate knowledge, a special kind of knowledge, information about God and eternity. Recently, however, some pulpits have discovered that this very definition of words, that is, as signs to point to verifiable information, has made highly questionable the legitimacy of even using the word "God." Suddenly feeling trapped, some have unwisely reacted in antiscience belligerence while others have silently tossed in the towel. On the other hand, there are signs here and there that the church is discovering it is neither antiscientific nor antiintellectual to refuse to abide by a single definition of the function of words. No longer overawed, the church is discovering that science also has its limitations. After all, the "schemata which science evolves in order to classify, organize, and summarize the phenomena of the real world turn out to be nothing but arbitrary schemes...which express not the nature of things, but the nature of mind."[8]

In the opinion of some observers, a third reason for the current wordsickness lies in the changed shape of the human sensorium as a result of television. According to this interpretation, the visual has removed the oral from the field, or at least has created a crisis between eye and ear. The pulpit has traditionally used word and story and history, but now television has reorganized the sensorium for image and picture. In the opinion of some, the success of the Christian proclamation depends on the church's ability to make the transition so people can *see*. Against such a view, however, it should be kept in mind that the Bible favors the ear over the eye in attempting to present its message about God who communicates. If it be objected that this can be explained by reference to the Bible's primitive context, one should remember that in the same primitive context, the Hellenists gave ascendancy to the eye. Perhaps the difference can be explained by the fact that the Hellenists were concerned with the static conditions of the nature and being of reality while the Judeo-Christian interest was in the dynamic activity of God.[9] In a way unequalled by any of the other senses, the ear receives the temporal sequence of sensations appropriate to the communication of activity and the unfolding of the history of a people. One has to raise the question whether there is involved here something so fundamental to the Christian faith that, television to the contrary, the oral must remain in the center of the field of Christian proclamation.

Whatever conclusion one reaches on this point, no one could be more affected than the preacher by the changes in the structure of the human psyche and the shifts in the areas of sensitivity within the modern person's sensorium. If the capacity for receptivity is no longer polarized around sound and person but rather around sight and object, the difficulties for the preaching task are all too obvious. Perhaps the expression "God is silent" really is a reference to the deafness of modern humanity.[10]

That changes in the human sensorium have taken place in the past is well documented in Western civilization. Consider, for instance, the effect of the invention of alphabetic script and movable type on humanity's relation to the world and to one another.

> Writing and print created the isolated thinker, the man with the book, and downgraded the network of personal loyalties which oral cultures favor as matrices of communication and as principles of social unity... Inevitably, record-keeping enhanced the sense of individual as against communal property and the sense of individual rights. With printing, even words themselves could become property, as the principle of copyright came into being and was finally taken for granted.[11]

With the minimization of the socializing effects in voice and sound, individualism came into its own. The universe grew silent with the development of a literal culture. The spoken word came to be regarded as a modification of the written rather than vice versa. The understanding of the Bible, coming as it does out of long oral tradition, was radically altered. Words fixed in space by print tended to create the idea that the meanings of these words were fixed also. As a result, the written word was more authoritative than the spoken. What was read in a book was accepted as true, while serious attention to spoken words waned. If a speaker is really serious about what she is saying, let her "put it in writing."

The question is, of course, where does an oral presentation fit into a civilization that has moved from oral to literal and now perhaps to aural receptivity? Or does it? Is there reason to believe that the human voice, with its personalizing and socializing effects, has never really lost its place in our culture, and now in a mechanized and impersonal world, is more than ever longed for and needed? To this question we will return in a later chapter.

We have been considering possible causes of the present degeneration of language, a fact that is a contributor to the decline of the pulpit. Perhaps our discussion of the sickness of words should conclude by hesitantly entertaining the possibility that the reason is more profound, transcending all our analyses. This may be a time in which God has actually grown silent, weary with so many empty and careless uses of God's name. If so, surely healing and recovery of meaning will come out of such silence. But people keep talking, and "when God is silent, man becomes a gossip."[12]

A fourth cause of the current sag in the pulpit is the loss of certainty and the increase of tentativeness on the part of the preacher. Rarely, if ever, in the history of the church have so many firm periods slumped into commas and so many triumphant exclamation points curled into question marks. Those who speak with strong conviction on a topic are suspected of the heresy of premature finality. Permanent temples are to be abandoned as houses of idolatry; the true people of God are in tents again. It is the age of journalistic theology; even the Bible is out in paperback. The transient and the contingent have moved to the center of consciousness.

Basic to this feeling of temporariness and the attendant loss of certainty (whether it be cause or effect in relation to other factors is not of consequence here) is the shift of the church's concern from space to time. The traditional space-consciousness was fundamental to the church's proclamation, its evangelism, and its relation to culture. The church saw her task as that of increasing her place, her territory in the world. Now the church is more and more concerned with time. Pulpits are announcing what time it is: "the time is fulfilled."[13] The entrance of time, change, and flexibility means the exit of old forms of certainty and fixity.

This almost frightening awareness in our time of the contingency and creatureliness of all things pervades every serious grappling with reality and meaning. Philosophical studies have experienced a radical shift from considerations of Substance to those of Being and Time. The process philosophy of Alfred North Whitehead and the natural evolutionary eschatology of Teilhard de Chardin not only create but reflect the thought of our age. The most significant recent theological formulations have been to some extent structured on existentialism, which insists that the only path from thought to reality is through existence, my existence, with all the variables of my experiences coloring the picture. In view of this, many have thought it most honest if they spoke only of that which was verified in experience and remained neutral and silent about metaphysics. If God is mentioned, it is either in the passive voice or only in terms, not of God's being, but of our experience of God's presence.

It is an error to blame theology for the powerlessness of the traditional pulpit language; we preach in a radically changed situation. "The traditional metaphysical understanding of reality is being replaced by the historical understanding of reality."[14] Sermons that respond to this change simply by turning up the volume fall fruitless to the ground. "The resultant anxiety and underlying insincerity show that faith has been disastrously changed into the work of appropriating the incredible." [15] On the other hand, some have sought to avoid the difficulties for preaching that have come with the radical historicization of humans by trying to secure an area for faith free from the contingencies of historical investigation. The call to live "by faith alone" seems at first to capture the essence of perfect trust since it does not depend on the authentication of historical evidence. As a matter of fact, however, this position is a high and beautiful nest, for while it is not dependent on historical verification, neither is it threatened by any new discovery.

Lest anyone feel that the conditions just mentioned are confined to the university world of discourse, let us look at modern art. Whatever may be one's aesthetic judgment, this art reflects the breakup of old perspectives with their confident delineations of reality and captures the fragmentation that accompanies rapid change. Or look at modern architecture. Churches do not look like churches any more! Church architecture captures the flexibility and changing structures of our world while celebrating trust in a God of the present. Within such buildings, a neat three-point sermon is highly suspect. In a world such as this, what right have preachers to impose a symmetry that they alone can see? Or do they? Every work of art, music, or literature of our time has suffered the loss of neat and isolated beauty because the shadows of once remote cruelties and injustices are brought by modern communication media to fall across every page and every easel. While these shadows remain, and while the reality we experience continues in transit, the old art forms will be inappropriate and inadequate.

> In this sense modern music is the product of a radical tentativeness become audible. The available acoustical possibility of sound and rhythm are [*sic*] used, not to declare one man's variations on an agreed consensus about the world, but to work out in sound and rhythm one man's behavior in a world without form.[16]

Amid all this, the sermons of our time have, with few exceptions, kept the same form. What message does such constancy of method convey? Either preachers have access to a world that is neat, orderly, and unified, which gives their sermons their form, or they are out of date and out of touch with the way it is. In either case, they do not communicate.

As a rule, younger ministers are keenly aware of the factors discussed above, and their preaching reflects it. Their predecessors ascended the pulpit to speak of the eternal certainties, truths etched forever in the granite of absolute reality, matters framed for proclamation, not for discussion. But where have all the absolutes gone? The old thunderbolts rust in the attic while the minister tries to lead the people through the morass of relativities and proximate possibilities. And the difficulties involved in finding and articulating a faith are not the congregation's alone; they are the minister's as well. How can she preach with a changing mind? How can she, facing new situations by the hour, speak the appropriate word? She wants to speak and yet she needs more time for more certainty before speaking. Hers is often the misery of one who is always pregnant but never ready to give birth. Is not every sermon delivered too soon or too late and hence a compromise of the commitment to speak the right word at the right time? Does not the fact that each sermon can, in the nature of its limitations, say only one thing and hence be partial in its content make the preacher a heretic every Sunday, under judgment for all left unsaid? Does the fact that the pastor's own faith is in process, always becoming but never fully and finally arrived, disqualify him from the pulpit? Not really feeling he is a member of the congregation he serves, he is hesitant to let it be known when his own faith is crippled for fear of causing the whole congregation to limp. It is this painful conflict between the traditional expectation of him and honesty with himself, a conflict so dramatically heightened in our time, that gives the minister pause and often frightens him from the pulpit.

A fifth reason for the current decline of the strong pulpit has already been touched on: the completely new relationship between speaker and hearer. There are many ways to look at this. One hears a great deal these days about the fall of Christendom, a fact sometimes lamented, sometimes celebrated. Whatever else it may mean, the collapse of Christendom means the church's loss of the scaffolding of a supporting culture. No longer can the preacher presuppose the general recognition of her authority as clergy, or the authority of her institution, or the authority of scripture. An examination of great evangelistic sermons of the past makes it clear that the speaker assumed at the outset that the hearers were part of a culture that was Christian and the appeal to them was simply not to be "holdouts." This condition is rapidly disappearing, and the claim of the gospel must be presented on its own terms with the understanding that the hearers stand amid several alternatives. In this respect, the fall of Christendom is to be welcomed by the preacher, for when assumptions give way, faith can be born. Unless there is room to say no, there is no room for a genuine yes. And yet it is apparent that the new situation in which preaching occurs is critical, and unless recognized by the minister and met with a new format, sermons will at best seem museum pieces.

Unfortunately, the physical arrangements for preaching make it difficult for the minister to implement the changed relation between speaker and hearer. The very location and elevation of the pulpit imply an authority on the part of the speaker or the message that the minister is hesitant to assume and the listeners no longer recognize. Not only this but

> the preacher looks down; the people look up. Often, as the lights in the church are turned down and a spotlight turned on the preacher, the congregation disappears into an identity-hiding gloom. The elevation of the pulpit lifts the Word of God above life, and would seem to contradict the concept of its embodiment in the life of the people. The arrangement, moreover, confirms the stereotype of the relation between clergy and laity in which the Word is removed from the people and made the preacher's exclusive sphere of responsibility.[17]

Many congregations, no longer passively accepting this stereotype, refuse to listen to the Word shared under this arrangement. The vigorous processes of democracy are under-mining high places, including pulpits.

The younger minister feels most acutely this changed relationship between speaker and hearer because of the nature of seminary education. The seminary experience has increasingly become one of seminars, discussion, and participation groups where all speak and all listen. Training in education, both in and out of the church, has warned minsters of the sterility of a setting in which one speaks and many listen. A minister thus educated entering a parish may feel equipped to function as pastor, counselor, and teacher, but may feel awkward and ill at ease in the pulpit. The minister may feel the appearance of the preacher in the pulpit is a contradiction of seminary experience and of the other aspects of ministry. On the continent, the education of ministers is still quite deductive, with all the built-in authority structures. To the extent that American seminary education has been dependent on the European, this has also been true here. However, the development of an American educational philosophy has produced a new breed of leaders. The conflict between the two modes of thought and the two perspectives on the speaker-hearer relationship has often appeared as a conflict between a minister (deductive, authoritarian) and the educational director (inductive, democratic), between sermons and adult education. It also appears within the young minister as a conflict within the self as preacher and teacher.[18] The preacher seriously asks whether it is best to continue to serve up a monologue in a dialogical world.

A sixth and final reason here offered to explain what is often called "the crisis in preaching" is not new at all, but is inherent in the very nature of preaching itself. Preaching lies within the general category of communication and therefore shares the painful difficulties characteristic of that category. "Talking," for most people, is relatively easy, but meaningful and important communi-cation is difficult for everyone. Thus, we understand why husbands and wives, fathers and sons delay indefinitely those important conversations. Thus, we understand ecumenical organizations' making great strides in "Life and Work" projects long before serious conversation about "Faith and Order" can get underway. Such sharing with each other is rewarding, of course, but it is also very demanding. Saying words can belong to the deepest level of human relationships. While there are those who hesitate to preach because preaching is "only words," there are others who hesitate because preaching *is* words. These are the ones who understand that any violation of even dull and insulting preaching is a felony of such magnitude as to justify a blanket dismissal of the pulpit. In fact, it just may be the case that the turning of some young ministers from the pulpit is strange and indirect testimony to the truth about Christian preaching: it is demanding, exhausting, painful, and, for all involved, creates a crisis, a moment of truth, a decision situation of immense consequence. Quite consistently, the scriptures declare that presenting the word of God effects a decision to accept or to reject. Read again the terms of Isaiah's ordination. The message will be effective: hearts will be opened and hearts will be closed; some will draw near and some will turn away. So are we to understand the strange words of old Simeon at the dedication of the infant Jesus: "This child is destined for the falling and rising of many in Israel" (Luke 2:34), and this is the frightening logic of the words of Jesus reported in John 15:22: "If I had not come and spoken to them, they would not have sin; but now they have no excuse for their sin."

Anyone who is a bearer of light is thereby the creator of the possibility of a new kind of darkness. Those who see themselves as bearers of the light of democracy and freedom must occasionally shudder at the realization that they are helping make room for the riot of excesses that freedom makes possible. Whoever carries the light of learning to dark minds can only hope that the new uses of the mind will be true and honest. It is possible to understand, if not sympathize with, Mahatma Ghandi's rejection of Frank Laubach's literacy program for India. He reasoned it would be better not to be able to read than to read the trash that would flood India. He was wrong, of course, because every person has the right to be fully human, and this means the right to choose for him- or herself. But it is disturbing to remember: "This is the judgment, that the light has come into the world, and people loved darkness rather than light" (John 3:19).

Wherever such sensitivity about the task of the pulpit prevails, there may be fewer preachers, but there will be more preaching.

As would be expected and hoped, there has been a variety of serious efforts to meet the problems that beset the pulpit and to bring about recovery of the power of preaching. These have effected varying degrees of success.

The most immediate and most natural response to the problem has been for some pastors and churches to call upon the seminaries for more homiletics. Surely more required hours in homiletics would correct the slippage! But where the homiletics courses offered were more of the same, by seminaries seemingly unaware that preaching in a changed context demands something different, not just something more, the result has been the solidifying of old errors. A variation of this quantitative approach has been the demand for more Bible and more theology. But in some cases there has been the charge that preaching is too full of Bible and theology; weaken the formula. Whereas individual tastes here and there have been satisfied by adjustments in "more matter and less art" or "less matter and more art," the general lift given the pulpit has been slight.

A more noticeable attempt to infuse life into the pulpit has been the revival of topical preaching, a form that, on the face of it, seems to allow more relevance, more contact with the daily press. Expository or biblical preaching has been found guilty of archaism, sacrificing the present to the past. One should, according to this view, choose relevant topics for treatment. Scriptures can be read in the service for mood or atmosphere or to satisfy those who feel they should be included, but they should not be allowed to shackle the minister.

Some marked improvements have been noted, with some real Christian sermons on current issues being heard. Preachers of smaller caliber, however, have been thus lured into forgetting that they have the right to preach, not because of what they get from the newspaper, but because of what they bring to it. Relevant sermons we all want and need, but what is painfully lacking is a mode of proclamation that is relevant to the present speaker-hearer relationship. Why is it that on occasion, when the topic of the sermon is relevant, vital, and interesting, the listener feels a poorly defined but very real resistance to all that is being said? The young prophet in the pulpit feels this resistance and extends the "prophetic" role to include the condemnation of those who do not go along with what's being said. Quite often the problem is in the method of preaching, in the downward movement of the sermon with an implicit view of the hearers that is not acceptable to them. Even the angry preacher, deliberately iconoclastic and anticlerical, preaches relevant sermons in a way no longer relevant. The preacher is still saddled with the traditional image of preaching with its clearly discernible authoritarianism being communicated nonverbally not only in intonation and manner but also in the form and movement of the sermon. The preacher may have radically rearranged the furniture and removed the lofty pulpit, but the distance between speaker and hearer is still successfully maintained by an arrogant, and perhaps learned, smirk. It may be that the old way of keeping the distance was easier to take.

In recent years a number of techniques have been employed to overcome a fundamental weakness in traditional preaching, its monological character. Without question, preaching increases in power when it is dialogical, when speaker and listener share in the proclamation of the Word. This fact has been understood by really effective preachers for a long time, but we have of late seen a host of new implementations. Some ministers have sharing sessions with laypeople prior to the final preparation and delivery of the sermon. A number of others have feedback following the sermon in a variety of formats. Efforts to build dialogue into the actual delivery have taken the forms of forums, dialogue between pulpit and lectern, press conference sermons, planned interruptions from the congregation, and other variations doubtless already familiar to the reader. Responses have ranged from mild enthusiasm to "at least it's different." Disappointment felt by preachers and listeners is probably due to the fact that dialogical methods are rather easily postured, while embracing the dialogical principle requires a radical reassessment of one's role as a preacher, one's view of the congregation as the people of *God*, one's understanding of whether the sermon is the preacher's or the church's, and one's theology of the Word; that is, does the Word of God occur at the lips, at the ear, or in the sharing of it? These are profound and complex issues, but they have to do not just with what is preached but how one preaches. This is the meaning of an earlier statement insisting that effective preaching calls for a method consistent with one's theology because the method is message; form and content are of a piece. A perfectly good sermon, contentwise, on "The Priesthood of All Believers" may in effect be contradicted by the method of presentation. And here method of presentation does not refer simply to the minister's attitude or disposition; it refers to the fact that the movement of the shared material may not allow the hearers room to be priests at all in any responsible sense.

This difference between method and principle of dialogue is extremely important. Reuel Howe has reminded us that

> a communication which in terms of method is monologue (one speaker) may at the same time be governed by the principle of dialogue; and similarly, although two people

may be addressing each other, if neither is responsible for or responsive to the meanings of the other, the communication is dialogue only in terms of method and lacks the dialogical principle.[19]

Multiplying references to the world as such hardly succeeds as a dialogue with the secular.

In much of the "new preaching," one can detect a longing, not just to be heard and understood, but to be accepted by a world that has been alienated by the religious jargon of a self-addressing church. The guilt for this alienation must be accepted and confessed. However, offering slang and fashionable jargon as "renewed" preaching, celebrating the secular embrace of certain Christian symbols (i.e., use of crosses as warnings at highway danger points, putting Christ in Christmas, etc.), or reducing the gospel to the lowest common denominator of acceptable faith and ethic will hardly be received by a serious world as adequate penance. The ease with which some ministers speak of the world's problems today arouses suspicion. Are these problems of unrest, injustice, and violence being addressed or celebrated? Franz Kafka's parable comes to mind:

> Leopards break into the temple and drink to the dregs what is in the sacrificial pitchers; this is repeated over and over again; finally it can be calculated in advance, and it becomes a part of the ceremony.[20]

Weaving an individual's pain into the litany hardly relieves the agony. Nor is it of real consequence for the future of preaching to spend time bragging on the world for its honesty, frankness, and integrity while clubbing the church for hypocrisy and pretension. This gross oversimplification is full of error, failing to see how people pretend irreligion as well as religion. The world gets no great lift from this dubious favor of having the Pharisee back away and beat his chest so the Publican can stand to boast of his pride. "In our effort to correct the monologue from the church to the world, let us not fall into the trap of substituting the monologue from the world to the church—that is, of offering it as the preacher's sermon."[21]

The renewal of preaching calls for something more than a different interpretation of our world, even if that interpretation be a correct one. We will know power has returned to the pulpit when and where preaching effects transformation in the lives of people and in the structures of society. There are reasons to believe that this renewal is not far away. We turn now to examine some of the signs that arouse this expectation.

CHAPTER 2

The Pulpit in the Spotlight

In the words of judgment against the pulpit are to be heard the first stirrings of new life for preaching. To be railed against is to be complimented; to be neglected is the final insult and the clear pronouncement of death. Those of us vitally concerned with preaching, perhaps possessed of unjustified hope, tend to interpret the measure of the depth to which the pulpit has fallen as also the measure of the height to which it should and can rise. Would so much time be given to general criticism of sermons if there were not among us yet a high expectation? Disappointment is registered only against a backdrop of expectation.

How is this general expectation of something vital, clear, and significant from preaching to be explained? Why do people week after week return to their hard chairs before dull pulpits to hear a preacher thrash about in a limbo of words relating vaguely to some topic snatched desperately on Saturday night from the minister's own twilight zone? Habit? In some measure, yes, but the sermons they have been hearing have been such as to break even the strongest addiction. The survival of the habit can be partially accounted for by the nourishment it receives from a subterranean hope: perhaps today there will be a word from God. This is a hope born of faith in a God made known through words. In a time when many speak of "mere words"so pejoratively, it may seem almost incredible that "words" would be a means of God's giving Godself to us. But over against this disregard for words is in our time a gathering of concerns and explorations into the meaning of language that has no equal in the history of our civilization. The simple and yet profound act of speaking with one another has become the center for a whole constellation of studies philosophical, theological, biblical, psychological, and practical.

Why this self-consciousness about language has arisen at this time is difficult to explain with certainty. The electronic age, with its offering of a wide variety of ways to present the human voice, has commanded new attention to oral language.[1] Perhaps the ascendancy of science and the domination of the scientific method have created such a restricted view of language that a reaction in favor of more dimensions to language is to be taken simply as clear testimony to a general degeneration of meaningful discourse, a degeneration in which the church figures prominently. Whatever the cause or causes, the fact remains:

> We can no longer take language for granted as a medium of communication. Its transparency has gone. We are like people who for a long time looked out of a window without noticing the glass—and then one day began to notice this too.[2]

It is difficult to miss the judgment against so many sermons that this attention on speech carries. It may be a correct observation that we have to become dumb again in order to learn to use words faithfully once more. But it is also difficult not to see in this concentration on words the raw material for new preaching with power and significance. What one hears *in* preaching may be discouraging, but what one hears *about* preaching is most encouraging. For example: "The word is something that happens, an event in the world of sound through which the mind is enabled to relate actuality to itself."[3] Or again: "Language enters into the history, personal and collective, of man and shapes it for better or for worse; it simultaneously creates understanding and incomprehension, it binds together and it rends asunder."[4] If only the possibilities in discussions *about* preaching could be realized *in* preaching!

So full of promise for the pulpit are current studies in linguistics, speech, hermeneutics, and communication that a brief sketch of these various approaches is here offered. The general importance of discoveries about the nature and meaning of human communication will be evident to the reader and will hopefully encourage the preacher. Perhaps one of the greatest needs just now is a "theology of speaking," a clear conviction about what happens in a speaking-listening situation. In a later chapter, suggestions for the appropriation of these insights and the translation of this theology into a method of preaching will be offered.

In the first place, it should not be assumed that modern studies of language are dances over the grave with hope of a resurrection. In our culture words are not altogether dead; signs of life appear in a number of ways in ordinary experiences. One has only to recall significant moments such as a baby's first word, a long-awaited telephone call, the few nervous words at the marriage altar, the heavy sentence of a judge, or one's name over the loudspeaker in a hotel lobby to realize anew how much of life is mediated and even constituted verbally. Perhaps more dramatic illustrations are found in hospital wards, where a visitor's warm hello turns on the light, opens the shutters, straightens the linens, and brightens the faces; or in rural America, where a major business transaction is sealed by one man's giving his word to another; or in the quiet guidance of Anne Sullivan, who with the one word "water" brought Helen Keller into the world of human experience; or in the nation-shaping speeches of Adolf Hitler and Winston Churchill. In all our relationships, though frayed and torn by suspicion and deceit, there remains the vestige of sacredness about one's word. To face the charge "But you gave your word" is to be condemned without excuse or appeal. In a sense, all a person has is her word. In certain moments of her life, she is asked to give it. If in those moments she is separated from her word, then she is separated from herself. She may gain many other words, big important words, words that will get votes, win compliments, elicit applause, gain members, or sell real estate, but having lost her own word, she herself is lost. Let no preacher feel embarrassed that she deals with words. Genuine words are the stuff of our life together.

Secondly, in addition to that importance attached to words that remains a vital part of our common experience, the fields of psychology and psychotherapy have been making us increasingly aware of the role of words in healthy personal and social life. And by "words" we do not here refer to printed or written words on a page that give us the isolated individual, alone with a book, separated from the community. Rather, we are referring to words in their original form, their purest form, words that pass orally from person to person, words in their native setting in the world of sound. If this perspective seems primitive and preliterate, it should be remembered that in the electronic age we have become increasingly sensitive to the oral and the aural. "Voice, muted by script and print, has come newly alive."[5] Written words tend to restrict communication to statements, information, and the increase of knowledge. Of course, this is not totally the case, but those writers who have sought to extend the power of written words beyond this limitation have done so by developing an "oral style," seeking to involve the reader in conversation. Novelists work diligently to make the written dialogues between characters in the story seem "real," that is, oral. Certainly the content of communication is important, but it is in *speaking* words that an event occurs that transcends the informational dimension of the transaction. Something happens, involving at least two people, because spoken words effect participation and communication. "The power of words as an event is that they can touch and change our very life, when one man tells another, and thus shares with another, something of his own life, his willing and loving and hoping, his joy and sorrow, but also his hardness and hates, his meanness and wickedness."[6] It is not surprising, therefore, that Marshall McLuhan, a communications theorist, has called speaking a "cool" medium. By this he means that not all is given by the speaker; much has to be contributed by the listener. Active participation by both is required.[7]

The vitally significant function of spoken words has been shown in work with the deaf. Pedagogical techniques have been developed for introducing deaf-mutes, indirectly of course, to the world of sound, because it has been established that if left unattended, the congenitally deaf are more intellectually retarded than the congenitally blind. Parallels are also to be found in the emotional problems of the deaf.

> The importance of auditory experiences for the interpretation of reality is proven through observation of deaf children…A world without sound is a dead world; when sound is eliminated from our experience, it becomes clear how inadequate and ambiguous is the visual experience if not accompanied by auditory interpretation…Vision alone without acoustic perceptions does not provide understanding. Deaf persons are prone to paranoid interpretations of outside events.[8]

Not only for the deaf but for everyone, silence distorts reality and eventually destroys emotional and social health. Each individual discovers herself and matures in relating to others. These fundamental and essential relationships are developed and sustained by words spoken. By means of the human voice, awarenesses are shared; by means of a common language, persons are bound into pairs, families, and communities. Words express and incarnate community. This fact is dramatically underscored when words cease, silence falls, and communication breaks down. A husband and wife cease talking with each other and into the gulf of that deadly silence rush suspicion, resentment, jealousy, and misunderstanding. The marriage is ended not only *in* silence but *by* silence.

Unlike written words, spoken words create and sustain among us a consciousness of one another and an openness to one another in trust. The reasons are obvious. Spoken words are by their nature dialogical, and in dialogue what one says is not fully predetermined but is in a large measure a response to the preceding comments of the other. The words are never all present at once as in a printed text; on the contrary, words as sound move toward a goal as yet undetermined. Again unlike written words, spoken words are never past or future; sound is always present, always an existential experience.[9] Thus, there is in the act of speaking a consciousness of movement, change, uncertainty, openness to interruption, and, of course, insecurity. This is true regardless of how carefully one screens and censors words as they pass from the lips.

Without script or rehearsal, words normally shared in communication are more or less spontaneous, open-ended, and revealing of more than was intended. As a result, with the ascendancy of the spoken word over the written in our electronic age, several developments have followed naturally. In the first place, an open-ended style of life featuring dialogue and discussion of issues, a lack of finality, and the spontaneity of conversation characterizes our way of life. Second, the value of open-ended discussion and conversation has been seen by those who seek to heal faulty self-images and broken relationships; hence, therapy by group dynamics as well as by one-to-one conversation. Third, the introduction of openness into the most interior areas of human life, those of faith and value judgment, is on the painful but steady increase in our society. Fourth, pedagogical method has been profoundly affected by the embrace of the spontaneous in the dialogical process. The instructor comes prepared and unprepared, willing to listen to what she could not hear in the privacy of her own study and to respond to it. And finally (for our purpose here), preaching has been affected by our movement into the oral-aural world. Inevitably, the pulpit has been revisited and reevaluated by psychologists, therapists, communication theorists, and, of course, by the preachers themselves.[10]

Although considerations of method will be delayed until a subsequent chapter, still it is apparent at this point that a change is called for. In a world oriented around printed words, the sermon competed for attention by seeking to possess the qualities of a written text: logical development, clear argument, thorough and conclusive treatment. In other words, the sermon carried the entire burden; the listener accepted or rejected the conclusions. Many great sermons of the past were ready for the press shortly after, or even before, delivery because these sermons were esentially unaffected by the contingencies of the situation. They spoke but did not listen; they were completed at the mouth, not at the ear. These sermons presupposed passive audiences, and because other ministers could also presuppose passive audiences, these printed sermons were borrowed for their own pulpits. A speech to an audience can be repeated in many places by many people with a minimal change in effectiveness; speaking with a participating group is unique to each occasion.

In the present atmosphere of open-ended dialogue, sermons in the classical tradition will less and less be accepted. This fact is unsettling to many preachers, of course, because in the traditional method, the preacher was safe, free from all the contingencies and threats of dialogue. Now to be effective, a preacher must expose herself to all the dangers of the *speaking* (rather than the *speech*) situation. She not only trusts her words to the hearers but opens herself to their response. She believes the sermon needs the hearers to be complete. Conversation is not an individual production. The event of the word of God needs the ear, for faith comes by hearing (Rom. 10:17).

This adjustment to the new atmosphere of the oral-aural world is or will be radical and painful for many who preach, for it demands an altered image of the preacher and of what he is doing when he preaches. Some may feel they have too much to lose to expose themselves; others may feel that to do so would be to sacrifice the noncontingent and authoritative nature of God's Word, which calls not for discussion but for decision. Perhaps so; we will have to discuss this later. If, however, the minister laments the loss of former clerical prestige due to the processes of dialogue, he has reason to celebrate the recovery of the sense of the church as community. The words *community* and *communication* must not lose sight of each other. In fact, "the renewal of the preaching ministry is the rediscovery of its communal character."[11]

We come now to the third of the converging lines of current study and investigation that put *word* and *speaking* in the spotlight and therefore offer fresh possibilities for new power in the pulpit. We considered first the residue of power in words in all social inter-course in spite of the abuse and degeneration of language. Next the central role of oral communication in personal and social health and in the formation of community was briefly noted. Now we turn to philosophy to survey several significant approaches to the problem of language and the nature of the experience of communication.

The meaning of words and the phenomenon of speaking are at present a preoccupation of philosophy. Approaches and conclusions differ widely, of course, but a general conviction among philosophers is that one of their primary tasks is to come to clarity about language, to analyze the uses of language to shed light on the major problems that always confront philosophy. This is not to say that this is entirely a new concern for philosophy. Precision and clarity of terminology is of critical importance for any respectable discipline. But beyond this, the phenomenon of speech has received special attention. For example, it is generally recognized that sound is the most immediate sensory coefficient of thought, and speaking is very closely related to thinking.[12] If thought is nested in speech, perhaps investigation would reveal an organic connection between the brain and the vocal folds. Such investigations were once vigorously pursued. Alfred N. Whitehead has called attention to the part of the body from which speech comes to help explain sound as the natural symbol for the deep experiences of existence.[13] Whitehead regarded speech as human nature itself without the artificiality of writing, which is a relatively modern phenomenon. He was prophetic of more recent perspectives on speaking in his well-known comment, "Expression is the one fundamental sacrament."[14]

Of the more recent philosophical investigations of language, there are, in the main, two approaches. One approach acknowledges the validity of the scientific method and its insistence that words signify meanings that are verifiable. This perspective is primarily concerned to eliminate nonsensical statements, or at least to distinguish between nonsense (unverifiable) and sense (verifiable). Under the pressure of this demand by logical positivists, those who speak and write in the field of religion have not only felt called upon to clear up the fuzzy and meaningless jargon that often characterizes their field, but many have relinquished all terms that refer to the unverifiable. In general, this means neutrality toward, if not denial of, the entire realm of metaphysics. Since the word *God* has been so long associated with metaphysics, it has in some quarters been abandoned.

An interesting and significant variation within this general approach to language is that of Ludwig Wittgenstein's linguistic analysis. Wittgenstein has insisted that no theory or perspective be forced on language but that it should be analyzed in its everyday use. Words and expressions are to be understood when they are at work, not when they are idling, because speaking is part of an activity, a form of life, and is to be understood within that context. To illustrate the importance of the "form of life" context for language, he imagined the situation of a lion suddenly using familiar human expressions. In such a case, there would be no meaning because of the radical discontinuity between the words and the form of life in which they were used. Wittgenstein classified various language settings and activities as "language-games."[15]

Wittgenstein's insight is important for the preacher to the extent that it liberates language from the restrictions of the single perspective of the scientific method. Wittgenstein is, however, still bound by the overarching principle of verification, and the preacher simply must refuse to be thus restricted.

> The search for verification, which is the essence of scientific method, is without a doubt a sign of intellectual re-sponsibility, but when it comes to dominate philosophy, it marks a failure of nerve. Life which is psychologically and philosophically healthy always ventures beyond certainty; lived meaning is never wholly verifiable. A philosophy which is at the service of the enrichment of life dare not become obsessed with the problem of conclusive verification.[16]

The second of the recent philosophical approaches to language is to a large extent an attempt to overcome the tyranny of the single perspective, to break the domination of empiricism and the insistence that words serve only as signs pointing to the discovered or discoverable data. With many convinced that words have a richer and wider range of power than can be understood in any single perspective, there has arisen a strong "primitive" movement in language study. This is an attempt to recover the power possessed by words before they were smothered by a scientific and technological culture; words that once rendered immeasurable services to the human spirit; words that danced, sang, teased, lured, probed, wept, judged, and transformed; words that joined hands artfully into analogies, metaphors, riddles, paradoxes, parables, poems, legends, and myths.

Of course, not all who are here called "primitives" are saying and doing the same things, but they hold at least two common convictions. First, there is the suspicion of speculative metaphysics with its terminology charting ideal or ultimate reality. Instead, the primary concern is human existence and the concrete, lived experiences of individuals and societies. This philosophical stance is both creative of and expressive of the general orientation of our time, although an existential preoccupation with the present is fading before a growing appetite for words about the past and especially about the future. Second, there is a general acceptance of the priority of words or speaking in the constitution and expression of reality. "Man is a speaking animal" is the beginning definition. Words are regarded as transcendent in that they create and give meaning to human experience against the background of mute nature. Jean Paul Sartre appropriately entitled his autobiography *The Words.* Georges Gusdorf, a leading French existential phenomenologist, has said that whoever finds and speaks *the right word* is involved in creation out of chaos, and whoever *keeps his word* creates value in the world.[17] In a similar vein, J. L. Austin has reminded us of the creative or "performative" power of words. Words not only report something; they do something. Words are deeds. Illustrations are shared abundantly: words spoken at the marriage altar, by the judge passing sentence, in the ceremonies of christening and knighting, to name only a few.[18] These examples of dynamistic and creative functions of language are the residue of a primitive view of the power of speech before words became impoverished.

A reading of one of a number of excellent surveys of the role of words in primitive societies[19] would help the preacher recover respect for the words she often handles carelessly. Such reading takes one into primitive cultures where magic dominates. Here one meets the power of a word to effect change in earth, sky, and humanity. In a way defying rational clarification, words were believed to contain something of the object for which they stood. Hence, a person's name was indissolubly linked to the person so that one's name was a property, to be carefully guarded and cautiously used. The survey leads to Egyptian and Babylonian creation myths, in which the precreation chaos is described as a time of the "unspoken," when there was no name for anything. Likewise in India, the Spoken Word was exalted above the gods, for on the Spoken Word all gods, men, and beasts depend.

And, of course, this study leads into the Bible itself. Here, too, it is the Word of God that brings order out of chaos, separates light and darkness, and produces the heavens and the earth (Gen. 1; Ps. 33:4, 6, 9). Humanity shared in this creation, taking physical and intellectual possession of the world by giving names to all living creatures (Gen. 2:19). Throughout the Old Testament, in ordinary or sublime statements, in magic or prophecy, Israel took as her starting point the conviction that a word possesses creative power.[20] Therefore, the Word of God is an event, a happening in history. Perhaps the most comprehensive, as well as one of the most beautiful, expressions of this understanding is found in Isaiah 55:10–11:

> For as the rain and the snow come down from heaven, and do not return there until they have watered the earth, making it bring forth and sprout, giving seed to the sower and bread to the eater, so shall my word be that goes out from my mouth; it shall not return to me empty, but it shall accomplish that which I purpose, and succeed in the thing for which I sent it.

Later Judaism, taking a philosophical turn in its dialogue with Hellenistic religion, came to speak of Word as a hypostatic entity separate from God, but mediating in the business of creating, sustaining, and guiding the world.[21] These speculations on the Divine Word were to be significant in forms of Hellenistic Judaism and in early Christianity. This could hardly have been the case had not ancient cultures provided the preparation, recognition, and appetite for such an elevated view of Word. The idea of the primary significance of Word was durable enough to survive transitions from philosophy to mythology and back again.

The spoken word is of such vital importance in the ministry of Jesus and the apostles and is so crucial for understanding the New Testament itself that a subsequent portion of this chapter will be devoted to it.

We are at present calling attention to the return by certain philosophers to primitive understandings of the spoken word in order to revive language smothered under the small heading of verificational analysis. Perhaps foremost among these primitives is Martin Heidegger. For Heidegger, language is not a bag of tools, a pile of raw material to be used by humans, the masters of their world. For him, the capacity to hear and speak language is primordial. In his later writing, Heidegger has become more passive, more receptive, more concerned with people as listeners and not so much with people as interpreters, for he has come to believe that Being itself comes to us in a "clearing-concealing" through language. In language, Being itself is at stake, not just our use of words to discuss Being. Language precedes humanity; language is the loudspeaker for Being. Reality is linguistically constructed, for language is "the house of being." Heidegger quotes Hölderlin as saying, "Therefore has language, most dangerous of possessions, been given to man… so that he may affirm what he is."[22] Language is, therefore, not only the supreme event of human existence, but the very being of humanity is founded in language. In short, humanity is a conversation.[23]

Naturally some critics of Heidegger feel that he has become too mystic in his view of language, that his turn to poetry as the clearest means of establishing humanity's being through the word represents capitulation in the philosophical quest. Whether or not this is the case will not be debated here. It may very well be that he has unwarrantedly blurred any distinction between "mode of being" and "mode of expression," actually replacing a metaphysic of substance with a metaphysic of sounds. Perhaps the more cautious W. M. Urban is to be followed here:

> Reality is in a sense, doubtless, beyond language, as Plato felt so deeply, and cannot be wholly grasped in its forms, but when in order to grasp reality, we abandon linguistic forms, that reality, like quicksilver, runs through our fingers.[24]

Whether one prefers Heidegger's or Urban's formulation of the importance of words is immaterial here; what is central is the recognized irreplaceable value of human speech in laying hold of and bringing to expression Life itself. The preacher can expect to hear nothing more humbling nor more elevating than Heidegger's affirmations concerning Being's coming to expression in words. It approaches, or is, a sacramental view of speaking, provided, of course, the speaker is a listener.

We pause to note that it is becoming increasingly obvious that our discussion is moving us farther and farther away from those exercises referred to as "getting up a sermon or "preparing a speech" and "giving a sermon" or "making a speech." Those expressions already seem gross and insensitive violations of the high task of which we speak, that of "saying the right word."

We come now to the fourth and last of the lines that converge on the pulpit and, potentially at least, elevate it into prominence: that of theological and biblical studies. Here again the speaking of the Word is the center of discussion. Preaching may not welcome all this attention from the scholarly world, but after years of being shunted to the back of the catalog under a few faded listings taught by "staff," such attention should provide occasion for celebration.

Theological and biblical studies are here considered together for two reasons. Historically they belong together because any discipline within the Christian orb must deal primarily with word, the word of revelation, the Word of God. Against a background of silence, in a world where men and women lifted hands of prayer to Silence, Christianity came announcing, proclaiming. Silence is broken by Good News. As Ignatius of Antioch expressed it, Jesus Christ is "his (God's) word proceeding from silence" (Magn. 8:2); "He is the mouth which cannot lie, by which the Father has spoken truly" (Ign. Rom. 8:2). It is inherent in the nature of the Christian faith that its adherents not keep silent. Theologians and exegetes are concerned about the word that has been and is to be spoken.

Secondly, characteristic of theology and biblical exegesis in our time is the focus upon hermeneutics. Two disciplines that have often in the past pretended lack of awareness of each other, dogmatics and exegesis, now share a preoccupation with principles of interpretation. And what is most significant from our present perspective is that this general concern with interpreting the word is not confined to the written word; it is in the spoken word that the interest is most keen. By "spoken word" we refer not only to the long oral tradition back of the texts of scripture, but the word spoken in the proclamation of the church today.

> For if its aim is, that what it has proclaimed should be further proclaimed, then the hermeneutic task prescribed by the text in question is not only not left behind when we turn to the sermon, but is precisely then for the first time brought to its fullest explication. The problem of theological hermeneutics would not be grasped without the inclusion of the task of proclamation; it is not until then that it is brought decisively to a head at all.[25]

In spite of the intramural scuffling over the extent to which preaching is theology and theology is preaching, there is a widespread acceptance of the inseparable relation of theology and preaching. Theology is responsible reflection on the proclamation. Expressions of gratitude and responsibility are due from each to the other.

Two men about whom theological discussions for the last three decades have revolved, Karl Barth and Rudolf Bultmann, entered into their monumental labors in the service of the sermon. That God's Word be a living word, a real summons of a real God to real persons, has been the central concern of both. To the differences between them in the achievement of this end some attention will be given in the next chapter, but these differences in no way abrogate for either their common subscription to the Later Helvetic Confession: "Preaching the Word of God *is* the Word of God."

Why this attention on the Word and preaching at the present time? It is in large measure, of course, the heritage of the Reformation with its concentration on the Word of God. This concentration inevitably conferred importance upon hermeneutics and proclamation. But this focusing of attention on the Word of God gave new prominence to the oldest nemesis of preaching: How can the distance—geographical, intellectual, psychological, and linguistic—between the scriptures and modern hearers be negotiated without the sacrifice of either? All the old attempts—allegory, levels of meaning, symbolism, literalism, mysticism—seemed unsatisfactory. Although warned by the heresy of Ebionism against sacrificing the present for the past, post–Reformation biblical scholarship let its course be determined by the most intensely felt need of the hour: a ground of authority from which to debate with Rome. The scriptures, against their own will, intention, and warning, became the "paper pope," with the result that the present was sacrificed, immediacy in preaching was lost, and congregations became accustomed to being sacrificed weekly on the altar of "sacred history."

During this period we learned more about the Bible than we had known, thanks to new biblical disciplines: literary, historical, textual, and form criticism. All subsequent Christian scholarship would be, and is, profoundly indebted to this period of scientifically critical biblical investigation. But the sad fact in the midst of it was that all this attention on the Bible moved it farther and farther from those with whom it was shared in lesson and sermon. A deep resentment and discontent began to emerge in the churches as many sensitive Christians rejected that "Divine economy" that the situation implied: In Bible times the people had God, but we have only the Book. No one can be content bearing the brunt of some cosmic joke that says, "You were born too late to be where God's action is." Imaginative preachers tried: "This morning let us go back to old Jerusalem," but the benediction burst the bubble, and the sanctuary doors opened on a world that looked precisely like it did prior to the sermon. Pentecostal movements arose, as they always do in such barren times, hopeful that the strong winds of God would blow the dust from the sacred book and sacred desk. On a more sophisticated level, liberal Protestantism refreshed weary spirits with the announcement that all those ancient obscurities in the Bible were really intended to say no more than that we should love, forgive, be charitable, promote justice, and usher in the brotherhood of man under the fatherhood of God. Some pulpits embraced this idea and momentarily came alive with new "relevance," but most preachers knew that major problems are not really solved by winking at them.

Then the existentialism of the early Heidegger seemed to provide the key to the problem of interpreting scripture meaningfully for modern hearers. It appeared now that preachers no longer had to choose between scriptural sermons or relevant sermons, thanks to the epoch-making work of Rudolf Bultmann. By existentially interpreting the New Testament, the texts could now be shared with immediacy and with the conviction that the *gospel* was being preached, not first-century prescientific perspectives on the world, demons, the abyss, descents, ascensions, and so on. The preacher had found a scholarly friend, no doubt about it.

However, there were areas in Bultmann's program that gave cause for anxiety. Why the preoccupation with Paul and John to the exclusion of much that is in the New Testament, however unappetizing? Does everyone have the right to frame a canon within the canon? Is what Paul says to modern people really what Paul said? In other words, what we see as myth did Paul see as myth? Would it not be more honest just to disagree with Paul than to make everything he said so existentially relevant? And why the almost abnormal fear of historical exploration into the career of Jesus? Certainly we are saved by faith, not historical legitimization, but does not opening the door to the contingencies of historical discovery make more, not less, room for unsecured faith? Making a place for faith beyond the support of historical research is also removing faith from the threat of historical research, which means security par excellence. But most disturbing of all was the specter of anthropocentricism. "Modern man," whoever he was, seemed to be the measure of all things; he took his chair first, then the biblical furniture was arranged accordingly. Something upon which Karl Barth had insisted seemed to be needed—the Word of God precedes us; certainly we interpret, but first we listen.

Interestingly enough, it was Heidegger again who offered help. In his later years Heidegger has focused more and more on language, not as a tool for apprehending and articulating Being and Truth, but language as it belongs to the nature of Being itself. That which is ultimate, Being itself, comes to expression in language. It is not a case of our understanding and then finding words; the words precede the understanding. Life for us is linguistically constituted; that one can hear and speak words is one's primary gift. If, however, Being or Reality comes to expression in words, then the primary posture of humanity is that of listener, concerned to know the reality that comes to understanding through words.

Applied to biblical studies and to preaching, a shift from Bultmann's approach is evident.[26] Here we meet the primary concern, not of understanding language, but of understanding through language. One does not begin with the idea that we have in the New Testament verbal statements that are obscure into which we must introduce the light of understanding; rather, one listens to the Word hopeful that it will shed light on our own situation that is obscure. The Word of God is not interpreted; it interprets. Here a radical reversal in the direction of traditional hermeneutics occurs. The goal of biblical study is to allow God to address us through the medium of the text.[27]

Three implications for the preacher need at this point to be fixed clearly in mind. First, if God addresses people through the text, the Word of God must, by its very nature, be spoken. The church is compelled by its own understanding of a God revealing Godself through words to share its message through the personal contacts affected most basically by the spoken word. The church is driven by the Word to achieve at all times maximum communication. The burden this lays on the preacher is obvious, but the point here is, she is not to see herself as stammering along in some peripheral exercise. In and out of the pulpit her primary business is to communicate. Let those who oppose the preaching ministry with phrases such as "the acts of God" and "salvation events" recall the role of spoken words within those events that gave them their character and the role of spoken words in sharing the benefits of those events. There is in our experience no event so profound as speaking one with another.

The second implication for the preacher from what has been said about hermeneutics is that he see himself first of all as a listener to the Word of God. Granted the extreme difficulty of this posture for the pulpit, its importance cannot be overstressed. The preacher has often seen the congregation as the listeners; they tune in on the broadcast. Sermons are prepared for them; scriptures are interpreted for them; God tells them what God wants them to do. The preacher retails what has been somewhere, somehow, obtained wholesale. But one hardly needs the new hermeneutic to know that prior to all meaningful expression is impression. Paul outlined the plan of world evangelization, beginning not with the preaching but with the listening. "Faith comes from what is heard" (Rom. 10:17). Robert Funk has succinctly expressed it: "He who aspires to the enunciation of the word must first learn to hear it; and he who hears the word will have found the means to articulate it."[28] But this is not new insight; the prophet of Israel reflected the same sensitivity when he wrote:

The Lord GOD has given me
    the tongue of a teacher,
that I may know how to sustain the weary with a word.
Morning by morning he wakens—
    wakens my ear
    to listen as those who are taught. (Isa. 50:4)

The third implication for the preacher is the underscoring of what has been said earlier: the primary and fundamental nature of word is spoken word. The spoken word is never an isolated event; it takes place where at least two or three are gathered together. It presupposes that which it also creates: community. Spoken words that do otherwise are disruptive and violate the very nature of the church. Paul so informed the speakers-in-tongues at Corinth (1 Cor. 12—14). Speaking is to be in love, he said, for, properly understood, speaking and love travel the same street—from person to person. The homiletical definition of love is communication. Spoken words also set in motion intellectual activity. The sounds mean something is going on; there is movement and change.

Spoken words thus belong, as our lives do, to time, not space. The Hebrew feeling for word is legitimate and sound: word means primarily the spoken word, not a lifeless record but an action, something happening.[29]

This recovery of the oral quality of words has stimulated lively new approaches to the scriptures, making "listening" a real possibility again. From the beginning, oral speech has not only had a primal role in the spread of the gospel; it had a theological significance as well. In contrast to writing, speaking is direct, personal, engaging, and demanding. In addition, speaking, unlike writing, is committed to the time being, existing only in the present. A spoken word is therefore precarious, without secure continuities with past or future. Spoken words were thus appropriate to the nature of Jesus' life, his announcement that the time of the Kingdom is now, and the terms he issued for discipleship.

Of course, the oral style of Jesus and his early followers eventually submitted to the need to preserve and to repeat correctly. Written records appeared.

> But even when the face-to-face rhetorical forms of the beginnings gave way to the conventionality of written records and letters, these are still characterized by a perennially dramatic element which goes back to the very nature of the Christian religion. The Christian styles tend to evoke or restore the face-to-face encounter.[30]

As discussed by Wilder, Ernst Fuchs has pointed out that Jesus wrote nothing and Paul wrote with reluctance. When Paul did write, it was as a speaker rather than as a writer. He repeatedly expressed regret that he was not present to speak in person and almost invariably spoke of his coming soon, to complete and to clarify.[31] Paul understood that the Word was not just a certain content of meaning but an act, from person to person, that did something, that effected change.

In view of these insights into the inseparable relation of the gospel and the forms of its communication, the preacher would do well to ask with Amos Wilder, "What modes of discourse are specially congenial to the Gospel?"[32] Wilder himself has offered invaluable aid in the pursuit of his own question by analyzing the modes and genres of New Testament discourse. In further detail Funk has analyzed the parable and the epistle as oral speech.[33] It will not take a lengthy exposure to such studies of the lively modes of discourse used by Jesus and the early Christian evangelists to cause the average preacher to look upon her own standardized sermon outline with a new lack of appreciation. When she begins to ask herself why the gospel should always be impaled upon the frame of Aristotelian logic, when her muscles twitch and her nerves tingle to mount the pulpit not with three points but with the gospel as narrative or parable or poem or myth or song in spite of the heavy recollection of her training in homiletics, then perhaps the preacher stands at the threshold of new pulpit power. When he ceases to wail about preaching being sick and confesses that *his* preaching is sick, then the preacher will be willing to do something constructive: not simply choosing more controversial topics and more clever titles to divert attention from his monotonous method of outlining, but choosing a mode of discourse appropriate to the content to be shared and the experience he hopes will occur.

It should be said that there is no attempt here to imply that significant and fruitful insights into preaching are limited to Protestant scholarship. Prior to and especially in the wake of the attention to preaching in the Second Vatican Council, Roman Catholic contributions are numerous and noteworthy. Thomas Aquinas' dictum, "The primary duty of the priest is to preach the Word of God," is circulating again, and to render the new preaching more effective, excellent studies in the theology of preaching are appearing.[34] As would be expected, these studies are following those lines that must be considered if room is made for a strong sense of the significance of preaching: church and scripture in preaching, the faith and character of the priest and the efficacy of preaching, Word and sacrament, and the perennial problem of archaic language. Most of these issues are not peculiar to the Roman Catholic church, of course, but they are addressed vigorously within that fellowship. The central issue is, what happens in preaching? Is there an effective grace operating here or are the contingencies too great to speak with certainty about anything happening? In other words, is preaching a sacrament? There seems to be at present a tendency to speak of preaching as sacramental in the sense that Christ is present speaking his Word, but not a sacrament in the sense of *ex opere operato*. Preaching lies very near the sacrament and is to be understood as opening mind and heart in faith to receive the sacrament. But since the Word is effective in itself, the function of preaching is not merely preparatory. Unlike the sacrament, the contingencies related to the speaker and the hearer assume greater significance in defining what takes place. Hence, the priest who preaches must give attention not only to the Word of God, as though repeating sacred words would in itself be efficacious, but also to the words of people. The Word of God comes in the ordinary vernacular; hence, the priest is responsible for choosing his words and preparing carefully his sermon. This view of preaching is incarnational: as the Word came in the flesh, so the Word comes in the form of human speech.

This statement about the general direction of Roman Catholic studies in preaching is unjustly brief, but it is given with a strong urging that the Protestant minister read in this area. It may be that the sacramental and incarnational approaches will aid her in dealing with the primary question in her own preaching ministry: what happens in the preaching event itself?

This particular essay is suggesting that it would be fruitful if the minister would explore the profundity of the ordinary experience of conversing, talking, listening-speaking. It is not illogical to look for the God-person encounter within the channels that are already available and are already serving the most human experiences we have. And by no means should speaking be disparaged because it is so "everydayish." That same criticism could be leveled against the Bible, Jesus of Nazareth, and the church in her better moments. Is this not the point of it all?

> "Do not say in your heart, 'Who will ascend into heaven?' (that is, to bring Christ down) or 'Who will descend into the abyss?'" (that is, to bring Christ up from the dead). But what does it say? "The word is near you, on your lips and in your heart" (that is, the word of faith that we proclaim). (Rom. 10: 6–8)

We have surveyed the several lines of scholarship that converge on the pulpit today and provide the minister with adequate raw material for the framing of a theology of preaching that will not only withstand the current ridicule of the pulpit but will perhaps effect improvement sufficient to silence it. Perhaps this attention upon the primacy of the spoken word has prepared us to hear the word of Jesus in this regard.

> For out of the abundance of the heart the mouth speaks. The good person brings good things out of a good treasure, and the evil person brings evil things out of an evil treasure. I tell you, on the day of judgment you will have to give an account for every careless word you utter; for by your

words you will be justified, and by your words you will be condemned. (Matt. 12:34–37)

In Matthew's gospel this strong teaching regarding the eternal significance of what one says is prefaced by an even stronger one: the passage concerning the unpardonable sin (Matt. 12:31–32). This statement has served as a cannon to blast every foul and loathsome sin that ever crawled up into the human heart. Most likely the passage circulated in the early Christian community in defense of the function of the Christian prophet whose preaching was in the Spirit, announcing the Word of the Lord in a given situation. But what is surprising and awesome here is that the one sin placed by the New Testament beyond the reach of forgiveness is a sin of the mouth: "But whoever speaks against the Holy Spirit." Set against this text, the worn expression "mere words" steals away in embarrassment.

We move now in Part Two to a series of considerations related to a method of preaching that seeks to heed the warning and implement the insights that have been shared.

PART II

A Proposal on Method

CHAPTER 3

Inductive Movement in Preaching

For a number of reasons, a word of explanation and perhaps defense of this portion of the book needs to be offered. In the first place, this consideration of method may appear to some as discontinuous with Part One simply because traditional seminary structures have implied that "practice" stands apart from the main core of academic work. Has not everyone held the private opinion that "Practical Theology" was either not practical or was theology? Second, there is a commonly held notion that the rescue of the pulpit cannot come at the "level" of method. This implies, of course, that method is without depth, deals only with symptoms, and in general is to be classified as a skill achieved by training, not an understanding gained through education. Why embarrass the university community with courses on preaching when there is a good Toastmasters Club downtown? And finally, a sensitivity about method as such that amounts to an aesthetic reaction against this entire area of discussion is strongly represented in our culture. To ask, "How is it to be done?" seems so proletarian, so mundane, almost vulgar. Those who ask such questions would put shoes on larks, and chop the forest into firewood.

Response to these attitudes draws upon experiences that make sympathetic understanding possible. However, at the risk of being repetitious, it should be emphasized that the separation of method of preaching from theology of preaching is a violation, leaving not one but two orphans. Not only content of preaching but method of preaching is fundamentally a theological consideration. For example, the point of contact of the sermon with the hearers is an issue long and fruitfully debated by Karl Barth and Emil Brunner and occupying a foremost place in historical theology. Does one address oneself to those dark of mind and heart, or is the sermon designed to awaken people's "memory" of their true destiny? The answer affects how one communicates, verbally or nonverbally. Or again, why are there often in the pulpit such affected tones and gestures? It is not a problem of hand and mouth alone; it is theological and theologically to be resolved. When the preacher comes really to believe in the incarnation, that God comes to us in the ordinary, that God's Word comes in the usual patterns of the vernacular, she will trust that God can use the local idiom. Until then she will offer up "red letter" editions of herself, a mystery to her frustrated speech teachers. Nothing has so clearly documented the inextricable relation of method and content as has the recent work on the parables by Ernst Fuchs, Amos Wilder, and Robert Funk. Rather than being distilled for their content, the parable communicates *as parable;* it is the method that effects the experience. The method is the message. So is it with all preaching: *how* one preaches is to a large extent *what* one preaches. Looking ahead to what is yet to be discussed, it is not just the destination but the trip that is important.

The theological issues involved in method are innumerable. How one communicates is a theological commentary on the minister's view of the ministry, the church, the Word of God, sin, salvation, faith, works, love, and hope. And it is probably a clearer and more honest expression of one's theology than is the content of sermons.

As to the aesthetic reaction against the task of considering method, this is a pain with which the minister has to live, a pain shared with every writer, painter, musician, or other artistic spirit. In fact, that minister who feels every sermon is in a sense a crucifixion between the sky of intention and the earth of performance is a preacher to be heard with profit. But this pain is not to immobilize the minister. Every artist knows that palette and brush may compromise a vision, and yet to refuse to paint is to confuse purity and sterility. But it is also a delightful discovery that, once at work, the activity of doing the job often stimulates the mind to greater vision and clearer insight than can ever be known by those who passively protect their untried ideals.

So it is that articulation is as important for the speaker as for the hearers. By expressing her thought she becomes more thoughtful; by searching for words to give eyes to the listeners, she herself comes to see more clearly. Some preachers have theological terms for defining this experience, but all who share it know that speaking is such a bosom companion to thought and feeling that the separation of method from content is not only artificial but unfruitful.

One further introductory word: this essay proposes a method of preaching. While the guidelines suggested may inform a variety of sermon shapes, this in no way implies that the method discussed here is *the* method. In fact, forms of preaching should be as varied as the forms of rhetoric in the New Testament, or as the purposes of preaching or as the situations of those who listen. The one who trumpets "Reveille" *every* Sunday should not be surprised that the congregation ceases to believe a new day dawns; the one who sounds "Taps" *every* week should realize that the listeners do not really believe the curtain of life has fallen.

Anyone who would preach effectively will have as a primary methodological concern the matter of movement. Does the sermon move and in what direction? Movement is of fundamental importance not simply because the speaker wants to "get somewhere" in the presentation but because the movement itself is to be an experience of the community in sharing the Word.

There are basically two directions in which thought moves: deductive and inductive. Simply stated, deductive movement is from the general truth to the particular application or experience, while induction is the reverse. Homiletically, deduction means stating the thesis, breaking it down into points or subtheses, explaining and illustrating these points, and applying them to the particular situations of the hearers. Everyone recognizes this as the movement of sermons in the mainstream of traditional preaching. This movement is not native to American soil but is as old as Aristotle and to this day prevails in Europe,[1] from where it has been mediated to American seminaries and pulpits.

The assumptions that underlie the deductive movement of thought begin to appear when one looks at the form of outline on which it hangs.

I.

    A.

        1.

            a.

            b.

2.

a.

b.

Notice that the main point is given first and then broken down into particulars. In other words, the conclusion precedes the development, a most unnatural mode of communication, unless, of course, one presupposes passive listeners who accept the right or authority of the speaker to state conclusions that he then applies to their faith and life. And this is precisely the authoritarian foundation of traditional preaching, whether that authority be lodged in the church, the scriptures, the ordination of the clergy, or in the exclusive ability of the clergy by virtue of their training to handle aright the eternal truths. This relationship between speaker and hearer prevailed as long as Christendom as such prevailed, and therefore this was the movement appropriate to it. To have placed more responsibility on the listeners, to have left alternatives open to them, to have permitted their response to be the conclusion, would have been to create panic and insecurity, and thus to totally frustrate the flock. And, it might be added, there are quarters within the church where this would be true today. But the patterns of thought traffic have radically changed and continue to change. Recent discussions of preaching among Roman Catholics make this abundantly clear. As early as 1949, Viktor Schurr took a position against Karl Barth, saying that Barth's view of preaching was too authoritative and did not invite the hearer to participate in the sermon. Since the Second Vatican Council, Schurr's position has gained wider hearing. Wilhelm Weber has lamented the embarrassment and downgrading involved in the older method of deductive preaching to a world invited to a dialogue. And more recently, Bruno Dreher has called for "homiletical induction" that begins with an interpretation of human existence today and then moves to the text.[2]

Look again at the skeleton structure above. There is no democracy here, no dialogue, no listening by the speaker, no contributing by the hearer. If the congregation is on the team, it is as javelin catcher. One may even detect a downward movement, a condescension of thought, in the pattern. Of course, this may or may not appear in the delivery, depending on the minister. Some sensitive and understanding preachers modify the implied authority in a variety of ways: by voice quality, humor, or an overall shepherding spirit that marks all their relationships. But even here, a critical eye may detect a soft authoritarianism in the minister's words to those most obviously dependent upon her. Sometimes a term of affection may be a way of reducing another to a child, or a nonpersonal status. One may recall with what devastating warmth African American men were once called "boy" or "uncle."

Another glance at the deductive outline reveals a very serious obstacle to movement in the sermon: how does one get from 2b to main point II? That is a gulf that can be smoothly negotiated only by the most clever. Looked at geographically, a three-point sermon on this pattern would take the congregation on three trips downhill, but who gets them back to the top each time? The limp phrase, "Now in the second place," hardly has the leverage. She who has had the nerve to cast a critical eye on her old sermons has probably discovered that some sermons were three sermonettes barely glued together. There may have been movement within each point, and there may have been some general kinship among the points, but there was not one movement from beginning to end. The points were as three pegs in a board, equal in height and distance from one another.

It should be pointed out that some who preach have continued by bent of training and habit to outline their sermons as shown above, but in delivery have departed from it. The reaction against the pattern has been almost instinctive, as though such a structure violated the experience of communicating and the sense of community to be achieved. Some have even felt guilty about the departure, feeling they had ceased preaching and had begun to "talk with" their listeners. Lacking a clearly formed alternative, shabby habits and undisciplined and random remarks have been the result of this groping after a method more natural and appropriate to the speaker-hearer relationship that prevails today. Such casual and rambling comments that have replaced the traditional sermon can hardly be embraced as quality preaching, but the instincts prompting the maneuver are correct.

Perhaps the alternative sought is induction. In induction, thought moves from the particulars of experience that have a familiar ring in the listener's ear to a general truth or conclusion.[3] Locke Bowman, Jr., in explaining different teaching methods, sketches the difference between deduction and induction in the following fashion:

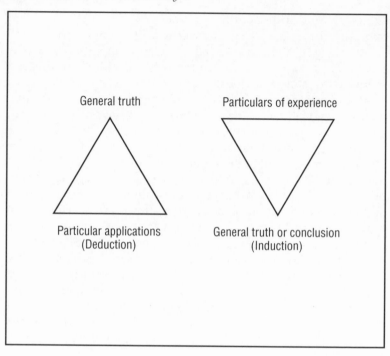

As Bowman points out and as the reader has probably already observed, much thinking and speaking consists of these two triangles stacked to form an hourglass: One moves inductively to a conclusion and then deductively in the applications of that conclusion.[4] However, induction alone is here being stressed for two reasons: First, in most sermons, if there is any induction, it is in the minister's study, where he arrives at a conclusion, and that conclusion is his beginning point on Sunday morning. Why not on Sunday morning retrace the inductive trip he took earlier and see if the hearers come to that same conclusion? It hardly seems cricket for the minister to have a week's head start (assuming he studied all week), which puts him psychologically, intellectually, and emotionally so far out front that usually even his introduction is already pregnant with conclusions. It is possible for him to recreate imaginatively the movement of his own thought whereby he came to that conclusion. A second reason for stressing inductive movement in preaching is that if it is done well, one often need not make the applications of the conclusion to the lives of the hearers. If *they* have made the trip, it is *their* conclusion, and the implication for their own situations is not only clear but personally inescapable. Christian responsibilities are not therefore predicated upon the exhortations of a particular minister (who can be replaced!), but on the intrinsic force of the hearer's own reflection. For this reason, the inductively moving sermon is more descriptive than hortatory and more marked by the affirmative than the imperative, with the realization, of course, that the strongest of all imperatives is a clear affirmative that has been embraced. Our society hardly knows any clearer contradiction of good sense than that of a speaker assuming a conclusion that is hers by hard work or inheritance but nonetheless hers alone and, on the basis of that conclusion, filling the air with "must," "ought," and "should," thinking thereby to produce sincerity, kindness, love, repentance, faith, and finally enthusiasm for the next gathering for more of the same. Her hearers, a group usually including family and good friends, are torn by frustration, embarrassment, apathy, hostility, and pity. Exhausted by her own fruitless efforts, the preacher alternates between writing "Ichabod" over their heads and "Golgotha" over her own.

The inductive process is fundamental to the American way of life. There are now at least two generations who have been educated in this way from kindergarten through college. Experience figures prominently in the process, not just at the point of *receiving* lessons and truths to be implemented, but in the process of *arriving* at those truths. Because the particulars of life provide the place of beginning, there is the necessity of a ground of shared experience. Anyone who preaches deductively from an authoritative stance probably finds that shared experiences in the course of service as pastor, counselor, teacher, and friend tend to erode the image of authority. Such preachers want protecting distance, not overexposure. However, these common experiences, provided they are meaningful in nature and are reflected on with insight and judgment, are for the inductive method essential to the preaching experience.

Fundamental to the inductive movement, therefore, are identification with the listener and the creative use of analogy. There are no strict rules to guide the preacher in the choice of analogy from the viewpoint of logic; he will be guided by the nature of the experience he wishes to provide in the sermon as well as by the destination he has in view. Analogies not only make an idea vivid but "through analogies we integrate our experiences into our learning. Casually we solve innumerable problems in our daily living simply by comparing them to similar situations we have already experienced."[5] The sermon enlarges and informs this experience by providing analogies drawn from the lives of others, those about us and those who belong to history. Of course, from a strictly logical viewpoint, no amount of analogy, however appropriately selected and arranged, constitutes conclusive proof in argument. This is, in the opinion of some, a fatal flaw in the inductively woven fabric, and to this matter attention will shortly be given.

It cannot be overemphasized that the immediate and concrete experiences of the people are significant ingredients in the formation and movement of the sermon and not simply the point at which final applications and exhortations are joined. Recall again the parable that lies at the heart of Jesus' preaching. Here the whole of life is concentrated into one concrete situation. Jesus does not make a call for faith in general but in relation to a specific life situation. The subject matter is not the nature of God but the hearer's situation in the light of God. The mundane concreteness of the parable is to be taken seriously as such and not as though it were the shadow of the real, an illustration of some "spiritual" realm. Everydayness is inherent in the parable because everydayness constitutes the locus of human destiny.[6] If one is not Christian here, then where? If not now, when?

A hesitation, almost a fear of concreteness, runs through the history of the church to the present day. We never cease being surprised that on the death of a saint, visiting mourners discover at the saint's home brooms, detergents, ironing board, worn sweater, trash can, toilet tissue, a can of tuna, and utility bills. Perhaps a fear of "thingification" has produced this unwillingness to admit concrete and specific things to the credit side of the sermonic ledger. If things appear, they are often robbed of their identity by being made illustrations of some transcendent good (the apple is round, forming a circle, the symbol of eternity, and all that). We need to listen to the psychiatrists speak of the "therapy of the bare fact." For a person mentally ill and confused, there is healing by just coming into the presence of real objects, ordinary identifiable things.[7]

The plain fact of the matter is that we are seeking to communicate with people whose experiences are concrete. Everyone lives inductively, not deductively. No farmer deals with the problem of calfhood, only with the calf. The woman in the kitchen is not occupied with the culinary arts in general but with a particular roast or cake. The wood craftsman is hardly able to discuss intelligently the topic of "chairness," but is a master with a chair. We will speak of the sun rising and setting long after everyone knows better. The minister says "All people are mortal" and meets drowsy agreement; he announces that "Mr. Brown's son is dying," and the church becomes the church.

Perhaps by this time the question has been raised as to the theological presupposition back of this conviction that the experiences and viewpoints of the listeners constitute a part of the experience of the Word of God in the sermon. If so, it should be said first that if the preacher is addressing the church in her sermon, she should recognize them as the people of God and realize that her message is theirs also. She speaks not only to them but for them and seeks to activate their meanings in relation to what she is saying. And yet, increasingly the problem of unbelief is within as well as without the church and to this the minister offers not just reprimand but an honest expression of that very unbelief: "Lord, I believe; help my unbelief." It is always best to be honest with one's own and another's situation. Pretending faith or lamenting the lack of it may impress an occasional unobserving visitor, but it is pure straw to the flock.

In the second place, it is theologically basic to the inductive method that, even in missionary preaching, the listener not be viewed as totally alien to God and devoid of Godwardness. This is not to forget that humans are sinners contradicting and resisting the Word of God nor to approach them as though each had a religious faculty to be developed. But neither are we to forget "the light enlightening every person," "the law written on the heart," or the *imago dei*, however distorted it may be. Bultmann's explanation of Paul's anthropology in Romans 5 and 7 captures the both/and nature of humans: we have a "memory" of our true destiny, but our ability to achieve it is perverted. Because of humans' perverted self-understanding, they do come into conflict with the Word of God, but a point of conflict is also a point of contact. Even a perverted relationship is a relationship; were there no relationship, there would be no conflict.[8] The inductive method operates on this assumption, that people do ask the question of their own being and of their relation to Ultimate Reality. To ask a question is to imply understanding, but to ask is also to imply lack of understanding. As Gerhard Ebeling has put it, "Only a man who is already concerned with the matter in question can be claimed for it."[9] Such is the condition of the listener: one who can hear and one who is to be heard.

In establishing the point that the congregation is, in inductive preaching, more than just the destination of the sermon, two matters essential to inductive movement have been stressed. First, particular concrete experiences are inherent in the sermon, not just in the introduction to solicit interest, as some older theories held, but throughout the sermon. On the basis of these concrete thoughts and events, by analogy *and* by the listener's identification with what she hears, conclusions are reached, new perspectives are gained, decisions made. This experienced and experienceable material is not to be regarded simply as illustrative any more than a person's life is to be lightly handled as an illustration of something. This is the stuff of the sermon, and its reality lies in its specificity. This is biblically sound procedure. Read again the Old Testament and note its almost embarrassing specificity. So it is in the New. Paul never wrote: "To whom it may concern: Here are some views on the slavery issue." He did write: "Dear Philemon: Let us talk about Onesimus." The incarnation itself is the inductive method. From experiences with the man Jesus of Nazareth, conclusions about God were reached, usually after painful revision. It is regrettable that sermons about Christ have too often reversed this procedure, as though Jesus had said, "Whoever has seen the Father has seen me," rather than, "Whoever has seen me has seen the Father" (Jn. 14:9).

The second matter thus far stressed as fundamental to induction is movement of material that respects the hearer as not only capable of but deserving the right to participate in that movement and arrive at a conclusion that is the hearer's own, not just the speaker's. The conclusion does not come first any more than a trip starts at its destination, a story prematurely reveals its own climax, or a joke begins with the punch line. Perhaps it will not be taken as irreverent to say that the movement of a sermon is as the movement of a good story or a good joke. It may also be compared to the movement of conversation around a table. We have names for those who announce upon drawing up a chair exactly where the conversation is going and with what conclusions, just as we do for those who insult us by explaining the joke and telling it again.

It is no small advantage of this type of movement that it creates and sustains interest, and it does so by incorporating anticipation. Life that is healthy and interesting moves from expectation to fulfillment repeatedly. Of course, sermons that offer expectation without fulfillment can be as cruel as sermons that offer fulfillment without expectation are boring. Both poles are essential to life and when in healthy tension, there is joy. In fact, the greatest single source of pleasure is anticipation of fulfillment. The period between the parents' announcement of a family trip and the trip itself may be the children's greatest happiness. All of us know there is something about the chase that is a joy apart from the catch. It is this dimension that makes Christmas. Rouse a person on a given morning and say, "It's Christmas!" and even if it is, to her it is not. She has not anticipated it. The saddest day of Christmas, therefore, is Christmas day. Another analogy: have a meal catered, depriving the nostrils and digestive juices of the anticipation whetted by the odor from the kitchen, and the stomach will resent it. And it will let its resentment be known. Again: watch an old man peel an apple for his grandson. Forget the sanitation problems and watch the deliberate care in beginning, the slow curl of unbroken peel, the methodical removing of the core. The boy's eyes enlarge, his saliva flows, he urges more speed, he is at the point of pouncing upon grandfather and seizing the apple. Then it is given to him, and it is the best apple in the world. Place beside that small drama a sermon that gives its conclusion, then breaks it into points and applications, and one senses the immensity of the preacher's crime against the normal currents of life. The Bible always has its "already" and "not yet." The announcement by the early Christians that the expectation of a Messiah was fulfilled went on to explain that the fulfillment was the basis for a new expectation. He has come; he will come. The absence of this expectation from a tired existentialism that absolutizes the Now made it inevitable that a theology of hope would arise to correct it. This correction is not only justified biblically; it is necessary experientially. If today's thinking about life and about the church is time-oriented rather than space-oriented, then by all means let the sermon reflect this orientation by moving, open and expectant.

This leads us to a third and final comment about the inductive method and the role of the listener: the listener completes the sermon. This has been implied already but needs elaboration because it is on this point that much of the criticism of the inductive method is focused. Now, it is customary to say that the congregation completes the sermon, but usually what this means is that the preacher has told the people what has to be done and then they are to implement it. What is here suggested, however, is that the participation of the hearer is essential, not just in the post-benediction implementation, but in the completion of the thought, movement and decision making within the sermon itself. The process calls for an incompleteness, a lack of exhaustiveness in the sermon. It requires of the preacher that she resist the temptation to tyranny of ideas rather than democratic sharing. She restrains herself, refusing to do both the speaking and listening, to give both stimulus and response, or in a more homely analogy, she does not throw the ball and catch it herself. This is most difficult to do, for any preacher full of his subject wants to possess and control not only the subject but all who hear it, lest it fall to the ground. He wants a guarantee that the word will not be lost between himself and his congregation. It requires a humility and a trust most of us lack to risk not having this control, to be willing to participate in sharing a matter that is bigger than speaker or hearer and which they can only explore together in wonder, humility, and gratitude. The subject that can be exhaustively handled in a sermon should never be the subject of a sermon. And yet how many sermons one hears in which the impression is given that the preacher had walked all the way around God and had taken pictures.

But the temptation to imperialism of thought and feeling can be resisted. The good artist is able to do so. A work of art does not exist totally of itself, but is completed by the viewer. Nothing is more disgusting than some religious art that is so exhaustively complete, so overwhelmingly obvious, that the viewer has no room to respond. It is this room to respond that also marks a good drama. Playwright Edward Albee said in a television interview that anyone who bought a ticket to see one of his plays had to assume some of the responsibility for that play.

Let us return to the parable. C. H. Dodd has defined a parable as

> a metaphor or simile drawn from nature or common life, arresting the hearer by its vividness or strangeness, and leaving the mind in sufficient doubt about its precise application to tease it into active thought.[10]

The parable as such would be contradicted and destroyed by being explained and applied. The effectiveness of much of Jesus' preaching depended not simply on the revelatory power of his parables but also upon the perceptive power of those who attended to them. "Let anyone with ears to hear listen."

This same expectation of humans' reaching out, of their responding as the completion of communication, characterizes the entire biblical story of God's relation to people.[11] One could almost characterize God as reticent to be obvious, to be direct and hence to overwhelm, even when people called for some clear and indisputable evidence from heaven. Whether or not an event was divine revelation depended not only on the objective factors in the event but on what one brought to that event. It was no different in the ministry of Jesus. The same occasion that moved some to confess faith in him as God's messenger elicited from others mutterings about the untutored Nazarene. In every situation some were sure God spoke to him; others said, "It thundered."

Those who walk away from the Word of God do so because they "will not," but they excuse themselves saying "I cannot." The preacher is moved by this "I cannot" and so begins to remove all obstacles in order to usher in faith: art, drama, and parable are fully explained, applications are complete, and exhortations are exhaustive. The poor listener, denied any room to say no, is thereby denied the room to say yes.

Thus far the attempt has been made to say that inductive movement in preaching corresponds to the way people ordinarily experience reality and to the way life's problem-solving activity goes on naturally and casually. It has been urged that this method respects rather than insults the hearers and that it leaves them the freedom and hence the obligation to respond. In addition, unfolding or unrolling the sermon in this fashion sustains interest by means of that anticipation built into all good narration. But granted a degree of merit in each of these considerations, several objections arise that are of some weight and are deserving of attention.

First, there is the immediate and obvious objection that the method here advocated opens the door to semipreparedness on the part of the preacher. She can offer up ideas in embryo or appear before the people with a few hastily gathered commas and question marks and smile reflectively over her inductive efforts. To the charge that this method pronounces a blessing over such lethargy there is really no solid refutation, at least no more than there is to the charge that deductive preaching provided the homiletical support for authoritarian and arrogant clericalism. If the inductive method is an umbrella under which the irresponsible and undisciplined can hide, it must make room for itself among a beach of umbrellas, for there are in the Christian ministry many hiding places. And how are these loafers to be flushed from their secure indolence without denying to the ministry that freedom essential to a strong pulpit and creative servanthood? Perhaps it is best to admit the strength of this objection but still choose the danger over its worse alternative. After all, there is no serious endeavor that is not soon made a game in the marketplace.

A second objection has more teeth: is there not something fundamentally unethical about the inductive method? Those who voice this charge look upon the traditional procedure of stating the thesis and dividing it into points as straightforward, "coming right out with it," while induction is sneaking up on the congregation and slipping in your biblical material when they are not looking. Now it has to be granted, of course, that there is no end to pulpit tricks and sneak attacks: the manufactured tear, public beating of the breast, slaying dragons on loan from the taxidermist, and thousands more. If the minister resorts to these, he will find in the inductive method some new devices for hidden persuaders, some new tactics for "getting them in the palm of his hand." But intrinsically, induction is no more unethical than a parable is unethical. It may shock a congregation long accustomed to packaged conclusions to find a decision on their hands, but it is never sneaky to leave a person room to choose. On the contrary, properly conceived, the inductive movement implements the doctrine of the priesthood of believers. Instead of paying lip service to this doctrine once a year on Reformation Sunday, why not incarnate it every Sunday in a method of preaching that makes it possible for the congregation to experience the awful freedom of that tenet? If, however, the preacher is only apparently leaving room for choice and conclusion, but in reality has left open only one door, then that process is to be defined by another term: deception.

In light of what was said earlier about achieving higher levels of interest for the hearers, it may be felt by some that herein lies a degree of treason, a compromise of truth in order to be interesting. This criticism asssumes that being true and being interesting are mutually exclusive; if a statement is interesting, it must not be true, and vice versa. This is insupportable. If the air is filled with bland abstractions about "righteousness" and "blessedness" and "redemption" because the truth must be brought out, the sermon is certainly not interesting and stands a fair chance of not being true. What is true does not always hurt or bore one to death, nor is it always true that what a person wants and what a person needs are different commodities. One should not feel guilt or compromise with the world if a parishioner expresses genuine interest in a sermon. The most penetrating analysis of the human condition with the clearest call to repentance can be interesting. Why? Because most of the people are not interested in ornamentation nor entertainment. They know where to go for that. They are interested in the removal of ornamentation and affectation in order to be intersected where they live. The old patter about those who dress up on Sunday to sit in church and play the hypocrite is out of date. The reverse is more true. It is the world that six days a week demands pretension and hypocrisy that has become a burden. These people come on Sunday hopeful of that which is becoming increasingly interesting these days: the truth, shared in a context where the push to impress and be impressed is absent. The fact that they chose to come to the sanctuary rather than elsewhere is clue enough for the preacher that these whose steady diet is cake still have an appetite for bread.

Before concluding these remarks on the ethics of the inductive method, let it be urged again that the preacher make not only the content but the method of sermons a matter of conscience and conviction. In a desire to permit listeners that freedom of choice that is essential for the birth and exercise of faith, the preacher may become guilty of equivocation. It may be with the minister as with the student who, unable to remember whether a word is spelled with *ie* or *ei*, forms both letters the same, places the dot between them, and leaves the instructor the freedom of choice! On the one hand are inhuman forms of confusion; on the other are the diseased forms of clarity and certainty. Between them lies the path of responsible preaching.

A third objection to the inductive movement of the sermon is theological and complex in its implications. It raises the question whether this method makes the Word of God dependent on the listener. Oversimply stated, is not the Word of God the Word of God *extra nos,* whether we hear it or not? Since the inductive method places so much responsibility on the ear of the hearer, does not this imply that the Word is the Word only when it is heard?

This issue should not be dismissed casually as no more than the old debate over whether a tree falling in the forest makes a noise if there is no ear to hear it. Important matters are involved, matters that lead one through the discussion by Karl Barth and Rudolph Bultmann. A major criticism of existentialism has been its loss of God's proseity, God's being and nature quite apart from and independent of our appropriation or understanding, replaced by theology that speaks only of God-*for-us* or *us*-before-God. The conviction underlying existentialist theology is that there is no direct path from the human mind to God; the path is through existence. This, of course, arouses the fear that truth will be debased to arbitrary taste, and that an overriding subjectivism will dismiss every item that is not viscerally authenticated. Are the long-treasured notions of correct teaching and orthodox tradition to go by the board so that there can be as many "truths" heard as there are listeners in the room?

These questions are vital and should give the minister pause. The matters can in no way be settled in the brief span of these pages. A few comments may help, however, toward fruitful pursuit of a solution.

In the first place, the charge that every listener hears a different sermon is simply an unnerving fact with which we all have to live. The only way to ensure purity of the message is to make it so dull that there will be no hearers awake to appropriate and distort. Actually, of course, there is no pure message any more than there is a pure noise; formal and informal interpretation go on all the time. The issue is how that interpretation is to be evaluated, positively or negatively. Is the appropriation of the gospel foreign to and in addition to its nature or is the appropriation of it inherent in its nature?

Certainly the gospel does not originate with the listener any more than music begins with those who attend to it. Of course, Christ is significant *extra nos*, but that significance is in his disclosure of himself to us. One's appropriation is not a distortion of the event but a part of its structure.[12] It is not a matter of saying truth is subjective, but it is a matter of asking whether there is truth inseparable from its appropriation. Whatever may be a person's theology of the Word as Truth complete and valid and final apart from all human grasp of it, the fact is, the person cannot employ such theology as a working principle for preaching. If he does, he will either identify his sermons with that Truth, and the messianism implicit in that identification will show itself in many alienating forms, or he will be reduced to silence out of fear of distorting or reducing the package of Truth before him. The fundamental error in this whole approach is the artificiality of the objective-subjective way of thinking. If the biblical text or the Word of God is objective and the human hearer is subjective, obviously the human is secondary, for the Word is the Word even if spoken into an empty room or into the wind.[13] But that is a contradiction of what a word is. Whether one views word as call (Buber), event (Heidegger), or engagement (Sartre), at least two persons are essential to the transaction, and neither is secondary. As Manfred Mezger has pointed out, an opera may be right and valid without an audience, but a service of the Word is a call, and a call is meaningless without a hearer. It is, therefore, pointless to speak of the gospel as Truth in and of itself; the gospel is *truth for us.* [14]

The gospel, then, is not a self-contained entity out there or back there that is narrated in its purity for ten minutes, with a final ten minutes devoted to milking lessons from it for us today. Those who hear are not just an audience; they are participants in the story. The pure gospel has fingerprints all over it. Recall how Paul understood the cross in the light of his suffering and understood his suffering in the light of the cross. Or again, God is addressed as Father because our experience has given the word meaning, but at the same time our experience of father is informed by the understanding of God as Father. It would be ridiculous to ask which part is the gospel and which part is application. Likewise it would be meaningless to ask if the Word is to be located at the mouth or at the ear; Word belongs to communication, and communication is listening-speaking-listening. It is in the sharing that the Word has its existence, and to catch it in flight in order to ascertain which part is of the speaker and which of the hearer is impossible nonsense. Let the words be spoken and let them go, trusting God who gave not only the Word but the gift of hearing and speaking.

> For revelation is antiphonal
> Nor comes without response.[15]

And if it be objected that this understanding of preaching not only shifts to the listener a portion of responsibility for the effectiveness of preaching but robs it of its thunder and authority, it should be asked again what constitutes an authoritative word. Is it any word blessed with a proper text? Is it the word voted unanimously at the annual assembly, or the word of one properly ordained? Or is it the word of some prophet without credentials who rails against the institutions and feeds the iconoclast in all of us? Many canons need to be applied, but in the final analysis, Dietrich Bonhoeffer was correct when he wrote:

> Someone can only speak to me with authority if a word from the deepest knowledge of my humanity encounters me here and now in all my reality. Any other word is impotent. The word of the church to the world must therefore encounter the world in all its present reality from the deepest knowledge of the world, if it is to be

authoritative. The church must be able to say the Word of God, the word of authority, here and now, in the most concrete way possible, from knowledge of the situation.[16]

A fourth and final objection assumes the form of a practical question prompted by concern for the mission of the church: does the inductive method of preaching effect change? Questions of strategy have to be asked by the church serious about her task in spite of the lurking dangers of utilitarianism.

This question about the inductive movement of the sermon draws its strength from two characteristics of the method: one, the inconclusive nature of inductive logic and, two, the apparent permissiveness in the hearers' being left to arrive at their own conclusions.

That induction is inconclusive from a logical point of view is clear. Doubt accompanies all induction. Its use of particular observations, analogy, and identification provides escape hatches that make uneasy those who try to negotiate life logically. Many who are more comfortable with deduction's tightly woven syllogisms often forget that their major premise was arrived at inductively or was taken for truth by virtue of the authority of its source. If the time comes, and it has, when people are either uninterested in those major premises of universal and general truth (i.e., "all people are unrighteous") or they question the authority of their source (i.e., church or scripture), those whose mission it is to convince others must go into the marketplace prepared to reason inductively. In a pluralistic society that is increasingly secular in outlook, people no longer hang on every word of a sermon that moves from "All people are unrighteous" through "You are a person" to a triumphant "Therefore you are unrighteous." Even within the church membership, one often meets questioners who want to know how the "first point" was reached, and more often one meets those who paid no attention to it.

The old sermons that roared along the second mile of universal and eternal truths without a single stop might document an interesting and in many ways great period in the life of the church. But the fact of the matter is, our generation is walking the first mile of primary data, the seen and the heard, and out of this raw material sermons are built. And this raw material often cannot be forged into major and minor premises. But so what? Only in mental institutions do we find those who live syllogistically. There one finds those poor creatures who have not "lost their minds"; they have lost everything but their minds. Some have impeccable logic; it is life that is confused and confusing for them.

If it is objected, then, that induction does not drive the hearers to the wall with its incontrovertible logic, the objection underscores a strength, not a weakness, of the method. If a situation is created in which the speaker and listeners are sparring, there are no winners, only losers, as hostility fills the room. The preaching experience should have as its aim the reflection on one's own life in a new way, a way that is provided by the gospel. If the sermon evokes this reflection, all the while bringing it into the presence of God, judgment and promise become actual doors open to the listener. The person who attends to such a sermon concludes for herself that the present condition is not inevitable nor irrecoverable. Nothing has been decided for her, but now with an alternative, she must decide. Now conditions are such as to make faith, which by its nature involves choice, a possibility.

All that those who sow the seed should ask for is this possibility. Who desires a world for a parish that is so devoid of freedom that only success is possible? It is a child's world, where there can be light without shadow, success without failure, yes without no. Jesus preached, and many walked away. That tense moment dramatized the frightening nature of freedom, but it also laid bare the nature of the decision of the Twelve. The *because of* and the *in spite of* were both present. Jesus invited a rich ruler to become his disciple. The man struggled with the alternatives before him and said no. It is a tragic scene, but it happens sometimes in a world where God has made it possible to say yes.

This leads us directly into the second half of the question raised about the effectiveness of inductive preaching: the issue of its permissiveness. Admittedly, the word *permission* sounds so casual, so unconcerned, that it seems to have no place in a discussion of our urgent business.

The truth of the matter, however, is exactly the contrary; permitting a decision and demanding a decision are two sides of the same coin. Permit persons to decide, and they are compelled to decide. Parents know this. It is extremely difficult for parents to back off to such distance as will permit the son or daughter to make a decision. This love act is not only permission but a demand, a burden placed on the young. Love also wants to protect them from the weight of this responsible freedom.

The plain fact is no one likes decisions. It is easier to relinquish one portion of one's life to the government, one to the school system, and another to the church. In the wake of this happy maneuver come many pleasantries: not making a wrong decision, not being responsible, and last but by no means least, criticizing all those stupid people trying to run the government, the schools, and the churches. Who has not, in the agony of deciding about an invitation to another post, wished a hundred times that the offer had not come?

But beyond our own discomfort before decisions is the pain of putting others in the position of having to decide. The preacher shares this hesitation and avoids it in a number of ways. Perhaps the method most common is to preach sermons that have the response built into the material. The "yes" response is built into sermons that echo popular prejudices and value systems or that tepidly announce that "Jesus was one of the great figures of history." On the other hand, and as a relief from the "yes" sermons, a "no" response can be woven into the material. Such messages assume in advance that the congregation will reject them and therefore the people are soundly condemned for doing so. This type of preaching has been called prophetic, and it is, if one has in mind the prophet Jonah. Jonah, assuming all would say no to his sermon, started the countdown. Bitterly disappointed, he refused to celebrate life because he had announced a funeral.

Certainly a decision is permitted; of course there is risk involved. This is no harmless undertaking by any means. But to risk everything is the only way to gain everything.

CHAPTER 4

Inductive Preaching and the Imagination

The inductive method of preaching makes such a demand on the imagination that the nature and the significance of that demand need to be considered in detail. If, as has been stated thus far, the preacher is to communicate in such a way that the congregation can hear what she has heard, she will not be satisfied to reduce the sights and sounds of her experience to points, logical sequences, and moral applications. She will fervently desire to recreate that experience and insight; she will seek to reflect it, not simply reflect on it. In this task, the preacher will be served best by what Martin Heidegger calls the primary function of language: letting be what is through evocative images rather than conceptual structures.[1] But we may be moving ahead of ourselves here. Perhaps our full appreciation of this idea and the role of imagination in preaching waits on our being disabused of faulty and inadequate understandings of this particular faculty of the human spirit.

Imagination is fundamental to all thinking, from the levels of critical reasoning to reverie and daydreaming. It is unfortunate and unfair that imagination has been popularly allied primarily with fantasy and thus often spoken of pejoratively as "just imagination" in the sense of the unreal and the untrue. Problem solving of all types, in the laboratory, in the kitchen, on a battlefield, or in the board room places a great burden on the image-making faculty of the mind. Our own age, committed as it is to facticity and to the literal sequences of printed words, can easily forget its indebtedness to imagination. Alfred N. Whitehead, scientist, mathematician, and philosopher, has described the path of human progress this way: "The true method of discovery is like the flight of an aeroplane. It starts from the ground of particular observation; it makes a flight in the thin air of imaginative generalization;. and it again lands for renewed observation rendered acute by rational interpretation."[2]

The galleries of the mind are filled with images that have been hung there casually or deliberately by parents, writers, artists, teachers, speakers, and combinations of many forces. The preacher knows they are there, and he knows they may or may not correspond to reality and therefore may aid or hinder communication and learning. For example, he knows that when he says "saint," an image appears that is very durable and most difficult to alter. If he goes on to speak of "a saint riding in an airplane," he should realize that saint and airplane are two very different images for many of his hearers and that they will relinquish one or both rather than admit his radical conflation of the two. It may privately satisfy the preacher to ridicule and scorn antiquated imagery, but the persistence of those old pictures is a tribute to the communicative power of previous generations and an indictment of his own inability to replace them.

Images are replaced not by concepts but by other images, and that quite slowly. Long after a person's head has consented to the preacher's idea, the old images may still hang in the heart. But not until that image is replaced is the person really changed; until then the person is torn, doing battle with the self and possibly making casualties of those nearby in the process. This change takes time, because the longest trip a person takes is that from head to heart.

All this is to say that in dealing with the imagination we are not on a tangent moving away from the center of the sober business of the gospel. We are, however, on a line of thought that moves against much common opinion. Recall how lightly pictures in a book are regarded in comparison to the script. Do examinations over a book include questions about the pictures?

> In a manuscript culture...very little exact information is deliberately communicated with the help of pictures, which, even when they contain exactly rendered representations of natural objects, tend to be decorative rather than informative in intent.[3]

Because images, in a book or in a sermon, are generally regarded as decorative and hence optional in their bearing upon the principal form and content of the communication, the imaginative preacher may have to endure such comments as "His sermons don't seem theologically weighty" or "It was too interesting to have contained much truth," or perhaps such inverted compliments as "I was much involved in your talk, or whatever it was. It didn't seem like a sermon." But the preacher will know what she is doing and will understand the power of an image to replace an image and hence to change a person or a society.

Imagination is as essential to life as is hope; in fact, the reactivation of the dimension of hope in theology has begun to bring about more positive reassessments of imagination. A significant little book appeared in the sixties with the title *Images of Hope* and the subtitle *Imagination as Healer of the Helpless*.[4] Imagination and hope belong together because imagination is inherent in hope. Hope has many images: a lion and a lamb lying together, breaking bread together, children beside a Christmas hearth, a banquet table, a bridal gown, a diploma, a pardon. No thoughtful person would toss these into a corner as "just imagination"; they are anchors cast within the veil.

For the minister, therefore, evocative imagery is not just an interesting introduction to a sermon nor a welcome break midway in the main body of the message nor a gripping conclusion. Images are not, in fact, to be regarded as illustrative but rather as essential to the form and inseparable from the content of the entire sermon. By means of images the preaching occasion will be a re-creation of the way life is experienced now held under the light of the gospel. Here imagination does not take off on flights into fantasy, but walks down the streets where we live. Here imagination reflects reality, and it is in their being real that sermons are rescued from dullness and impotence.

The place to begin discussing the function of imagination in preaching is not at the point of using imaginative words and phrases, but at the necessarily prior point of receiving images. As it is the person who hears who has something to say, so preaching begins not with expression, but with impression. This calls for a sensitivity to the sights, sounds, and flavors of life about one that is not easily maintained by the minister, or by anyone else.

Several factors are at work to close the pores of one's psychological and mental skin and effect the loss of sensitivity. This loss is in part a natural one, a poor bargain made in the process of maturing and growing older. William Wordsworth lamented for all of us the fading of those alert years when "the heart leaped up" at the sight of a rainbow or when eyes not yet dulled by dissipation could catch the "splendor in the grass." Physicist J. Robert Oppenheimer once said, "There are children playing in the streets who could solve some of my top problems in physics, because they have modes of sensory perception that I lost long ago."[5] All her life the minister needs to do battle against this gradual loss, for she knows that, as far as preaching is concerned, it is better to have a child's eye than an orator's tongue.

The battle can be waged with some success simply by staying alive personally. This means that the preacher does not allow herself to become only a dealer in those commodities that allow others to live; she herself lives. She does not just announce the hymns, she sings; she does not just lead in prayer, she prays. Time spent walking rustic lanes, pushing on crowded subways, strolling among window shoppers, or standing in dreary terminals where life is reduced to arrival and departure is not to be spent with notebook in hand getting illustrations for sermons. Rather, these are the movements and scenes of her own life and from her own psyche that inevitably become part of her preaching. If the imagery of her sermons is to be real, she must see life as life, not as an illustration under point two. This means that the preacher who sees a cloud as a cloud, garbage as garbage, a baby as a baby, and death as death will be able to share images that are clear and that awaken meaning. It is true that there are tongues in trees and sermons in stones but only the person who deals with trees as trees and stones as stones gets the message. It was while looking for his father's asses that Saul found a kingdom. Two men of Emmaus shared an ordinary evening meal with a stranger, and that supper became a sacrament. Life on its grandest scale comes to those who open the door to the ordinary.

This same open receptivity toward life mediated through literature will be equally rewarding in the effort to maintain sensitivity. Nothing is reflected more obviously in the content, mood, and dimensions of a preacher's sermons than the variety of his own reading. The most valuable literature for preaching is the great book read when the pressure of the next sermon is not there to turn the mind into a homiletical magnet, plucking usable lines from the page.

Of course, it must be admitted that some of the loss of sensitivity in the minister, or in anyone, is necessary for thought and concentration. To a certain extent becoming deaf and blind to distractions, a process often referred to as negative adaptation, is nature's way of enabling us not only to keep our sanity but also to earn a college degree, operate machinery, carry on a conversation, meditate, or get a little sleep. But even so, of all people, the minister should most often be asking himself, "In addition to that loud television next door, to what else have I become deaf?" Knowing the usual professional hazard of becoming hardened to the very human dramas that first moved him to the ministry, he will beware lest he add to it the conscious hardening that serves as defense against pain and loss. To be sensitive and open to others is to be vulnerable; that was made clear at the outset, at Golgotha.

By this time it should be evident how indispensable to preaching, and most especially inductive preaching, is the pastoral involvement in the life of the congregation. When the pastor writes a sermon, an empathetic imagination sees again those concrete experiences with people that called on all her resources, drove her to the Bible and back again, and even now hang as vivid pictures in her mind. When a pastor preaches, she doesn't sell patent medicine; she writes prescriptions. Others may hurl epithets at the "wealthy," but the pastor knows a lonely and guilt-ridden man confused by the Bible's debate with itself over prosperity: Is prosperity a sign of God's favor or disfavor?' Others may display knowledge of poverty programs, but the pastor knows what a bitter thing it is to be somebody's Christmas project. She sees a boy resisting his mother's insistence that he wear the nice sweater that came in the charity basket. She can see the boy wear it until out of Mother's sight, but not at school out of fear that he may meet the original owner on the playground. There are conditions worse than being cold. Others may discuss "the problem of geriatrics," but the pastor has just come from the local rest home and still sees worn checkerboards, faded bouquets, large-print King James Bibles, stainless steel trays, and dim eyes staring at an empty parking lot reserved for visitors. Others may analyze "the trouble with the youth today," but the pastor sees a fuzzy-lipped boy, awkward, noisy, wishing he were absent, not a man, not a child, preoccupied with ideas that contradict his fourteen years' severe judgment against girls.

Some ministers have conducted themselves on the principle that too much involvement in the lives of the parishioners constitutes an overexposure that weakens the force of their preaching. In other words, distance is essential to authority. In terms of one traditional view of the ministry, this observation is correct, but the inductive method cannot live with that image. In the inductive method it is essential that the minister really be a member of the congregation he serves. Some pastors seem unable, for reasons deeply imbedded in their own needs and fears, to live in this relationship with the people and hence to preach in this way. This is the meaning of earlier statements to the effect that one's method of preaching is determined by and is expressive of issues and convictions far beyond the province of a course in public speaking.

The danger for preaching that lies in open sensitivity to the experiences of others is not in an erosion of authority by overexposure, but in the overwhelming of the preacher's imagination. Having his mind flooded by the wide range and multiplicity of conditions of human need, he may make one of three errors in the sharing of images received. First, he may feel that so many needs face him that he cannot be specific and concrete in his sermons. To preach a sermon that re-creates and interprets the world of a teenager would be, he may feel, to neglect the elderly, or vice versa. Thus aware of all, he stretches the canvas of his mind to include everyone, and the pictures become vague and general and, hence, unable to evoke thought or meaning. Second, the preacher may, out of this concern for all the individuals before him, preserve the sharp, clear imagery of concrete situations, but crowd so many different pictures into one sermon that his kaleidoscopic presentation lacks unity, and lacking unity, it lacks movement. Both of these problems will be discussed in the next chapter. The third danger to preaching caused by an overwhelmed imagination is that of allowing the mind and therefore the sermons to dwell on the more spectacular, the more newsworthy images of the human condition. The news media now bring the world of violence, poverty, war, and moral debauchery to the mind on a wide screen, in color. The preacher will need to be careful lest his messages all become wide-screen and color presentations. While these conditions are with us and bear upon the meaning of being a responsible Christian regardless of how quiet and secure the local parish, it is also vital that the preacher not be seduced by television into thinking that these are the only needs in the world. There are many "meanwhile, back at the ranch" people whose needs are not only very real but whose conditions are worsened by the fact that they have been made to feel that, in a world as sick as ours, they have no right to cry for help. Many whose lives are small-screen, black-and-white, push through the crowd to touch the hem of His garment, hoping for a little inconspicuous healing.

The minister who is most capable of receiving and sharing the images that reflect reality is the minister who is not suspicious of any of her own faculties for such impression and expression. Some ministers, for theological or moral reasons, are not only suspicious of but are negatively disposed toward some dimensions of their own physical and psychic makeup. For example, quite a large percentage of the life pictures that come to us and ask to be reflected in our preaching are markedly emotive rather than logical or rational. A minister who is suspicious of emotion or uncomfortable with it will allow her preaching either to suffer the total loss of this flavor or to suffer the distortion of emotion by her poor translations of it into rational concepts. For this reason it is important for the minister to think through carefully her own estimation of those pathways in the human psyche along which people feel as well as think their way. This examination may raise the deeper but directly related questions about her own ability to cry or laugh or celebrate.

Some of us have been educated to regard emotion negatively, to define it as disorganized behavior or a biological lag. In the wake of this perspective came a view of maturity that was without emotion. The mature person served afternoon tea to both teams, but certainly never got caught up in the struggle. The result was a tourist-class citizen, negotiating life with a calm indifference, preferring to die curled up on some principle rather than to give his life fighting for what might eventually be judged an error.

This is, of course, a confusion of emotion and emotionalism, defining a quality by its extreme. Certainly there has to be clear recognition of the dangerous possibilities for dishonesty, deception, and maneuvering people by emotionalism. A preacher of integrity will avoid the practice of imitative magic, manufacturing tears, laughter, and other emotional signs in order to generate these among her hearers. On the other hand, such tricks by the charlatans should not effect the error of the opposite. In a simple figure, it is quite all right if the cup overflows, but the minister should not tilt it.

In our own time, the dominance of facticity characteristic of a technological age has tended to submerge the normal channels of emotional life, often producing abnormal and unhealthy emotionalism when it does surface. However, there are clear and welcome signs in recent years that we have learned anew that the presence of a full set of emotions is no evidence of the absence of intelligence, nor is the ability to feel strongly about a matter to be interpreted as lack of maturity. Effective preaching reflects the minister's open receptivity to those life scenes that are noticeably emotional in flavor but that constitute memorable and important stations along the way most people travel. From the time a baby reaches from the crib to catch the sunbeam streaming through a keyhole until the day when he sits old and alone among the pigeons in the park, the significant turns in the long road are marked by images with an emotional force that lingers in the memory long after the factual details are faded and dim. The preacher must be a whole person to admit such material without distortion or apology into his sermons.

We are considering the large room that belongs to imagination in every life with the obvious implication that preaching that moves inductively from concrete experience must not radically diminish that room nor alter it beyond recognition. This requires first of all an empathetic imagination in the preacher, a capacity to receive the sights, sounds, tastes, odors, and movements of the world about her. That this be real and not contrived necessitates receptivity to the full range of human emotion. Related to and yet possessing qualities beyond emotion is the aesthetic dimension of human experience. Sermons that reflect and address reality do not easily and always dissect every subject into true and false, right and wrong. Such divisions are also distortions because they are both partial and contrary to the way much of life is experienced. Many parishioners have come to expect, but still resent, the minister's reduction of life into the two categories—right and wrong. The reason for their resentment is that their experience has not been primarily one of right and wrong but perhaps could better be classified as the experience of beauty and ugliness. Should not the preacher include these categories if her sermons are to register the impression and the expression of reality?

Two objections may be raised against the homiletic embrace of the aesthetic. First, it may be argued that the aesthetic factors, while offering some interest and pleasure to the hearers, are, in fact, pure ornament and lack power to bring about any change. The urgent business of the Kingdom, we are told, demands that there be some leverage in all that we say and do, and beauty is powerless. Or to change the imagery, beauty is frosting, but it will not feed the world.

There is a practical ring to this position that is not without persuasion, nor precedent. It arises in church board meetings when the topic is carpets, steeples, stained-glass windows, and pipe organs. It arose when a woman "wasted" an alabaster jar of expensive ointment as she anointed Jesus at Bethany (Matt. 26:6–13). In a few minutes the aroma of that perfume had dissipated, and what improvement was there in the condition of the world? The disciples had a point: The ointment should have been converted to cash and the cash to blankets, bread, and milk for the poor. Is Jesus' defense of her, that she had done a "beautiful thing," really adequate? The world needs food, not fragrance. According to the usual canons by which people make judgments in the marketplace, Jesus stands corrected by any observant schoolchild. Should roses cumber the ground where onions will grow? How impractical and spendthrift is the aesthetic spirit! A choir of seventy voices works a total of more than seven hundred hours to prepare for a five-minute delivery into the air. That same amount of time and energy more practically directed would cut all the weeds along Interstate 35 from Wichita to Kansas City.

For all the wise caution and sound counsel in these clear-eyed observations, there still remains something essentially vulgar about this craving for utility. Whoever looks upon a forest as only so many feet of lumber, or upon clouds as only inches of rain, or upon meadows as only bales of hay operates the estate at a loss. Extract from a person's life a healthy portion of songs and flowers and you have reduced to something less than human "the creature the Lord God has made to have dominion over land and sea." This issue involved here is no less than the nature of humanity. That person who refuses to grow flowers because she cannot fry rose petals in the fat of swine is a person who would, upon embracing the Christian faith, turn everything to practical ends: prayers help insomniacs, Bible reading settles nerves, clean living and honesty pay dividends, and church attendance wards off communism. There is hardly any reason to preach to a man who would stand before a masterpiece in an art gallery with his hat on; he might hear the words but he would miss the tune of the gospel.

If the preaching of the church would address the whole person, then let the imagination play over the facts and awaken tired spirits. Many of the parishioners are not so much evil as they are bored, and their entire Christian experience has never provided them a chair in which to sit for an hour in the heavenly places with Christ. They do not need an argument; they need air. Why not sermons that celebrate the unconditional love of God? Instead of using Thanksgiving to scold the ungrateful, why not a doxological message? Instead of the weary harangues against commercialism at Christmas and the attacks against the once-a-year churchgoers at Easter, would it not be just as courageous to announce the Good News? Some Sunday mornings the minister should take the congregation by the hand and with them step off the dimensions of their inheritance as children of God. Some of them have been "preached at" for years but have never been given a peek into the treasury, much less the opportunity to run their fingers through the unsearchable riches of Christ.

Is it true that there is no power in such preaching? Certainly not! The power of a revolution resides in the spirit that approaches life aesthetically. The great champions of the Social Gospel application of the message of Jesus and the prophets to the industrial, social, and economic problems of America were people who looked at those problems with aesthetic sensitivity. The poetic spirit of Washington Gladden was violated by injustice and economic imbalance; the ugliness and stench of poverty and disease stirred to action beauty-loving Walter Rauschenbusch. And those now involved in the church's struggle against injustice would do well not to permit the aesthetic dimensions of the problems to be dismissed in the name of "stark realism." The social crises of our time are, among other things, conflicts of harmony and noise, symmetry and distortion, poetry and prose, beauty and ugliness, fragrance and stench.

The second objection to the sermonic embrace of the aesthetic is that such preaching does not speak to everyone. This position is predicated on the view that in the hierarchy of human values and needs, aesthetics is near the top and therefore beyond the experience of all but the cultured and leisure classes. These sober brows tell us that no preacher has the right to speak of beauty to the balconied few while the groundlings struggle with the soil for bread.

The facts themselves answer this objection. Humans in their struggle for survival have never been so reduced that their privations snuff out aesthetic life. Put them in the simplest cabins and they will plant petunias about the doors; drive them into a cave and they will play the artist on the wall; leave them nothing but sticks and they will devise flutes; bind them in chains and they will drag them to some remembered cadence; imprison them and they will sing hymns at midnight. The song leaders of America have been African Americans; what right have they to sing? Our country has been led in laughter by Jews who cannot remember when Israel did not have crepe on the door.

The preacher who shares the whole gospel with the whole person cannot listen to the guilt-laden people who weary us with their counsel that we cannot celebrate Christmas until Herod is dead. Of course the celebration is premature; all celebrations are premature. It is premature to sing carols at the crib when Good Friday is yet to come; it is premature to light birthday candles when death is one year closer; it is premature to kill the fatted calf when there is no guarantee the prodigal will not leave again. But Christ is born King even before Herod is dead. If in that harsh world a mother's whisper and a baby's cry could be heard above the clash of shield and sword, why should the preacher withdraw her own soft hopes and turn cynic? This is not to say that she will "use" aesthetics to infuse sweetness into bitter things. Rather, she will remain sensitive to those meaningful qualities of human experience that are often muffled by the sirens that daily alert the public to the beginning of a new countdown. The minister whose imagination receives and shares these sights and sounds will preach with a realism beyond that of a journalistic mentality.

We are considering the minister's capacity for impression as the necessary prerequisite for expression. An empathetic imagination means, first, having the wisdom and grace to receive the images of life about us and then, second, the freedom and confidence to reflect these with appropriate expressions. Such honest receptivity and reflection are fundamental to the nature and movement of inductive preaching, concerned as it is with the concrete realities within human experience. As we have noted, these experiences involve thought, emotion, and aesthetic appropriations. Finally, a word should be said about humor, because an honest reception of life's imagery will naturally and normally prompt laughter. The reason for this is that humor is directly related to the experience of concrete reality. The extent to which the preacher's mind dwells upon the general, universal, and abstract will be the measure of her lack of humor. Traditional deductive preaching, bringing general truths to bear upon the lives of the hearers, has therefore been marked by a lack of humor. But inductive preaching opens the door immediately to the presence of this dimension of our common life.

Inductive preaching will, therefore, have to face the criticism of often appearing less serious. Those who make such a criticism, feeling that the high seriousness of preaching precludes all humor in the pulpit, are more influenced by a Puritan heritage than by the Bible. They also fail to understand the nature of humor. Humor grows out of the genuine capacity to sense the seriousness or importance of an occasion, or an event, or a word. It is the person who is always apparently serious who is not really taken seriously. The force of humor as humor depends on the direct evidence of truth or significance in the matter involved. An analysis of humor will reveal at its base something sacred, profound, or highly significant. Hence, much humor involves occurrences in a school-room, in a sanctuary, in domestic relations, or in the attendance to creature needs. Even the sacraments of the church have provided occasions of humor, muffled, of course, by a sense of guilt that failed to see that only the true and meaningful can provide the leverage necessary for laughter. The human body knows this, because its physiological adjustments are essentially the same for laughter as for tears.

The raw materials for humor are the concrete realities experienced by all of us. Humor arises not when these realities are viewed nonsensically but when these are brought together with incongruity, effecting a misplaced accent, a slight distortion of the usual, or the mixing of values. Mary's little lamb at school, a bird in the sanctuary, a fly on the preacher's nose, a leak in the baptistry, a stubborn lock on the restroom door—these very concrete and experienceable occasions prompt laughter. There is no laughter in broad references to education, adoration, stewardship, righteousness, and humanity.

The minister who receives and shares the authentic signals of life as the congregation knows it will have a sense of humor. This does not mean he tells jokes. Telling jokes is no clear sign of a sense of humor and is a questionable pulpit practice with much common sense against it. But a sense of humor is simply the freedom to receive and to share life's imagery without the compulsion to evaporate the concrete into spiritual truths or melt it down into bland generalities. Thus understood, humor becomes for speaker and hearer a form of celebration, an expression of fellowship, a confession of trust in the Creator who made things as they are and who does not need the protection our humorless piety would afford.

Given, then, the capacity for being impressed by the full range of signals from life without and within, there remains for the preacher the task of expression. Simply put, this task is to use evocative imagery that will allow the congregation to see and hear what she has seen and heard. What she has seen and heard is not a special esoteric corpus of information about God that has been delivered to her to pass along, but our existence as it is in the liberating light of God's graciousness toward us. God's Word is not so much "a light which shines upon God, but a light which shines from him."[6] But how is the minister to speak so that the images she has received are formed in the imaginations of the hearers with clarity and force sufficient to effect changes in attitudes, values, and life directions? Perhaps the most adequate answer could be framed by distilling into several guiding principles what has been said or implied in this regard in this chapter and in the preceding ones.

First, let the selection of images to be shared be drawn from the world of experience known to the hearers and let these images be cast in forms recognizable as real and possible. This is to say, at no time are God's people to be given the idea that they are living at the wrong time, in the wrong place, on the wrong planet, to be really genuine Christians. It is a famous fault of preachers that they, perhaps to gain persuasive leverage, often draw on the exaggerated, the extraordinary, and the extreme image to portray the Christian life. The history of the Church is embroidered with real but rare dramas of martyrdom: Polycarp, Ignatius, and Joan of Arc did actually exist. But if the preacher makes normative the sacrifice of Polycarp, the conversion of Saul, the stewardship of St. Francis, and the service of David Livingstone, he will leave his most serious listeners wishing they were someone else, somewhere else. In the meantime, the Kingdom does not come to dull little towns where God's lightning never seems to strike. And the same is true in portrayals of evil. Nothing creates hypocrisy in the average church so much as sermons that succeed in identifying sin with those headlined crimes that plague distant cities.

Second, as far as is possible, let the preacher use words and phrases that image specific and concrete relations and responses. Each hearer is equipped with a set of senses with which to experience the world, and addressing those senses will awaken that experience anew. The minister would do well to check his sentences to see if his words convey that which can be heard or seen or smelled or touched or tasted. If the sermon deals with marriage, words that re-create the image of a particular wedding communicate much more than references to "holy matrimony." Holy matrimony does not reflect a single wedding ever experienced; it reflects on all weddings, and *all weddings* means to the hearers *no* weddings, just as *every*where means *no*where. If the sermon revives the memory of the odor of burped milk on a blouse, it evokes more meaning than the most thorough analysis of "motherhood." It is well to remember that much of the force of the sermon is dependent upon the preacher's sharing what the hearers already know.

Third, the principle of economy in the use of words, especially adjectives and adverbs, is invariably a sound one. The decision to do so is not simply in the service of brevity, but an economic use of words implements several principles of inductive preaching already discussed. The use of a few words suggesting the main lines of a picture permits the hearers to fill in the details and complete the image. This is their right and their responsibility as participants in the preaching. For the speaker to supply the total image robs them of this right, insults their intelligence, deprives them of a vital part of the process of arriving at new meaning and insight, and may well cause them to feel some revulsion toward the speaker. The reason is that detailed and complete description, especially of scenes of great joy or sorrow, reveals a lack of sensitivity in the speaker. Many ministers have gotten the opposite of their desired responses to very vivid and detailed portrayals of the Crucifixion. Communication, like revelation, must leave room for discovery. For example, no one ever directly reveals herself, but through specific attitudes, acts, and comments, observers are able to draw the portrait. This is the principle operative in the reaction of many Christians to the Fourth Gospel's reports of Jesus' sayings: "I am the bread from heaven," "I am the good shepherd," "I am the light of the world." These are better understood as conclusions about Christ reached by disciples than as his assertions about himself.

In this same vein, an economic use of adjectives and adverbs helps the preacher resist the temptation to tell people what to think in response to her comments. For example, if a speaker introduces a narrative illustration with such words as "I recall an event in the life of a very fine, genuine, outstanding Christian man," he has already told his hearers what conclusions to reach about the man: he is a fine, genuine, outstanding Christian. Why not tell the story about "a man" and upon its conclusion the congregation may say to themselves, "that man is a genuine Christian." In discussing the literary imagination, William F. Lynch has reminded us that "In tragedy the spectator is brought to the experience of a deep beauty and exaltation, *but not by way of beauty and exaltation.*"[7] Let the minister pile upon the people long sentences about the "inspiring and moving" and she thereby drains the occasion of all possibility to inspire or to move.

A final but not unimportant reason for not being complete and exhaustive in framing images for the listeners is that, had they actually been present to see for themselves what is being described, their experiences would have been partial and incomplete. Direct sensory evidence is never presented whole at a given moment, but is always fragmentary. No one has ever seen all of a chair or football or automobile at one time. If "being there" means fragmentary experiences, the preacher should know that exhaustively detailed imagery smacks more of unreality than of reality. It is a child's art that places both eyes on one side of the head to assure observers of the profile that the person portrayed had two eyes.

Effective words are set in silence, during which time the hearers speak. The real sermon is the product of all that is contributed by both speaker and listeners during their time together.

A fourth guiding principle for conveying to others images received is to avoid all self-conscious interruptions in narration and description. Dozens of times in sermons a minister may take his eye, and hence his listener's eye, off the subject by inserting such phrases as "we find," or "we see." Under no other circumstance does a person interrupt herself by telling those about her "we read" or "we find in this story." She just reads it and does not get between the book and those attending to it, unless, of course, she has an abnormal craving for attention. No one stands at a window with another and continually inserts distracting phrases such as "We are looking out this window" or "We see out this window." One simply points to the bird or the meadow or the cloud. Why, then, should these worse-than-useless, self-conscious phrases continue to weaken and scatter attention drawn by the preacher to biblical narratives or to the life scenes about him? These wordy encumbrances serve the sermon as effectively as a conversation would be served by the conversants saying frequently to each other, "We are talking."

A fifth and final principle to guide the effective sharing of images that awaken images is fundamental to the whole preaching task: the language used is to be one's own. There was a time when the language of the English Bible and the language of the marketplace and of the home were much the same. In fact, the English Bible was for many the basic text for learning and for teaching reading and writing, as well as for more advanced essays in the world of literature. In that time the minister's own language, that of the congregation, and that of the Bible were very similar.

Now this is becoming less and less the case. For the minister to fill sermons with biblical terms and phrases, assuming they have meaning, is to err tragically. In fact, it is a question whether there is in some of these terms real clarity of meaning for the preacher personally. One has come to expect to hear "blessed," "spiritual," "righteous," and "soul" in sermons, and they seem to caress the emotions of many, but little clear signification is conveyed. Some ministers and laity may continue an indiscriminate reciting of these words because they lament the demise of the Bible culture and the growth of secularity, but if the desire to communicate is strong, the lament will be cut short. There is no intrinsic value in simply repeating the confessional language of other people, even if their words are in the scriptures.

All this sounds very much as though the traditional language of the faith were being excised as an act of concession to modern ears untrained, untuned, and uninterested. The fact of the matter, however, is that this call for the vernacular in the pulpit is a call to obedience to Jesus Christ, who talked of the Kingdom of God in terms of borrowing a loaf of bread at midnight, worrying a judge to distraction with a civil suit, scrambling for seats at the head table, pulling bums in off the street to eat the king's banquet, and patching worn clothes. His refreshed hearers were happily amazed while his critics scored him for the clear absence of that jargon that often marks sermons off from all other human discourse. Dietrich Bonhoeffer once wrote:

> It is not for us to prophesy the day (though the day will come) when men will once more be called on to utter the word of God that the world will be changed and renewed by it. It will be a new language, perhaps quite non-religious, but liberating and redeeming as was Jesus' language; it will shock people and yet overcome them by its power.[8]

To refuse to use one's own language is to refuse to accept one's self, one's words, and one's hearers as an occasion for God. It is clear evidence of a lack of faith. But to offer up one's own words in the service of the Word is an act of full trust in God, whose power is made perfect in weakness.

Chapter 5

Inductive Movement and the Unity of the Sermon

The most important single contributing factor to consistently effective preaching is study and careful preparation. This must be said repeatedly in considering inductive preaching, because the method itself can so easily degenerate into casual conversation with the congregation. Since this method makes such large room for the particular experiences of the hearers, it is possible that some indolent preacher may choose this method as a recess from the books. The fact of the matter is that inductive preaching, because it has in it the possibility of easy detours and is so susceptible to prostitution, actually requires more discipline of thought and study. Confidence that sets one free to preach in this mode is gained in the same way one is confident and free in any method of speaking: know the matter being presented and be convinced of its importance. And it is a mistake to assume that the inductive method's embrace of the dialogical principle makes such preaching merely the tolerant exchange of differences and indifferences among sophisticated participants. Tolerance is there, to be sure, but like all sharing of the gospel, inductive preaching seeks to persuade.

There is, then, no substitute for careful preparation. When such preparation is lacking, the preacher gropes about in frustration for quick confidence to enable him to face the people. He may grab another preacher's sermon and handle it well, except for a hollow ring here and there and the subterranean sounds of his own soul crumbling in slow erosion. These sounds have bested the strongest arguments ever offered for filching sermons. Or he may turn to tricks and gimmicks in the pulpit, every Sunday leaping from the pinnacle of the temple, only to learn bitterly that he who begins with a rabbit out of the hat must soon come up with an elephant if he would hold his crowd. Or the unprepared minister may hide behind "style." If he happens to be blessed (or cursed) with easy words and immediate speech, he may use the high gloss of marvelous verbiage to blind hearers to the fact that there was nothing on the tablet. On the other hand, he may pass off a real or pretended crudeness of speech as the credentials of the prophet who does not come "with persuasive words of wisdom" but who humbly brings the treasure of the gospel "in earthen vessels." Some American politicians and pulpiteers have made capital of the anti-intellectualism in our society that accepts poverty as goodness, crudity as sincerity, and awkwardness as humility. Or the person facing Sunday morning without a message may sink into negativism. Her morning paper provides something to which she and all God's saints are opposed and so in five minutes she is prepared to oppose it for twenty minutes. The real dimensions of this tragedy are obscured by the popularity of muckraking, attacking vaguely defined enemies, and firing heavy mortar into empty buildings. But the preacher is not fooled by tactics; she knows she was called to build, and running a bulldozer over the lot once a week is hardly an adequate response to that call.

If the preacher is prepared, one of the clearest evidences of that preparation is the unity of the message. She will not try to corral several sermonettes hastily gathered under one title; perceptive listeners will be responding to a single theme that governed the selection or rejection of all material bidding for a place in the sermon. If the point has been made that the primary characteristic of forceful and effective preaching is movement, it should now be said that unity is essential to that movement. There can be no movement without unity, without singleness of theme.

The contribution to the movement and power of a sermon made by the restraint of a single idea can hardly be overstated. This may not be apparent at first to those who have struggled after enough "points" to make their sermons complete. Actually, the anxiety to get several points to serve as the basic structure for the sermon is paralyzing. It is better to forget about points. The question is, What is the point? Sermons that move inductively, sustaining interest and engaging the listener do not have points any more than a narrative, a story, a parable, or even a joke has points. But there is a point, and the discipline of this one idea is creative in preparation, in delivery, and in reception of the message.

In preparation, the imagination is released by the restraint of one governing consideration. Strange as it may seem, freedom blooms in confinement. Just as Saint Paul, John Bunyan, and Dietrich Bonhoeffer wrote most profoundly about freedom when the usual locomotions of apparent liberty were denied them, so the more confined the topic fixed in mind, the greater the freedom of mental range in pursuing and developing that topic. A broad topic or theme has no center of gravity; it draws nothing to itself, but sits alone on the page and stares back sterilely at the composer. But not so the precise and clear thesis. Like a magnet it draws potentially helpful material from current and remembered exposures to people and books. Because the preacher can state her point in one simple sentence, she knows the destination of the trip that will be the sermon. She knows where she is going. Made confident by this fact, a number of structures, or in a better figure, a number of avenues for the trip, begin to suggest themselves to an enlivened imagination. Some possible ways of beginning so that all the listeners can begin the trip together will appear. All the while, potential illustrative materials will be examined in the light of the central idea of the sermon. Whoever has this one governing theme in mind is in the enviable position of being able to reject a good story because it will not serve the purpose. A good illustration or analogy is an arrogant piece of material, mastering rather than serving. Unless carefully screened by a controlling thesis, a good story heard on Friday will take the spotlight in the next Sunday's sermon whether or not it has a place. It is the mark of sound preparation to be able to delay the use of good material.

Trying to assemble a sermon without the "releasing limits" of a single germinal idea is a deeply frightening and frustrating experience. Igor Stravinsky has written of his experience in the composition of music. First, he said, is the anguish of unrestricted freedom, but the experience of a creative freedom

consists in my moving about within the narrow frame that I have assigned myself for each one of my undertakings. I shall go even farther: my freedom will be so much the greater and more meaningful the more narrowly I limit my field of action and the more I surround myself with obstacles. Whatever diminishes constraint diminishes strength.[1]

In delivery, the limitation of the single idea is the key to forceful and effective unfolding of the message. The difference between a moving stream and a stagnant marsh is constraint. Such is the difference between sermons with and without the discipline of the controlling theme. In the process of delivery the difference is experienced by the preacher and detected in a number of ways by the congregation. The whole body—hands, face, eyes, voice—communicates the presence or absence of a clear sense of direction in the speaker. And the speaker knows it.

If there is not a single theme, all the energies that should have been harnessed to the one task are scattered and dissipated in the frantic search for a place to stop that will give the semblance of planning to this aimless wandering. Neither pilot nor passenger gets much from a trip that is made with landing gear down all the way.

And finally, in the reception of the sermon, singleness of theme contributes interest and meaning. One has only to recall the limitation of a forbidden tree in Eden, the midnight hour for Cinderella, or "high noon" in a popular Western drama to be reminded that it is boundary that arouses interest. It is the presupposition of the bounds of monogamy that draws readers' attention to stories of infidelity. Death is a great creative limitation in the affairs of each generation. The withdrawal of that restriction would be an unspeakable tragedy. So do hearers of a sermon sense very soon whether there has been careful restraint in preparation, whether some things will be left unsaid. If listeners know something will be left unsaid, they will contribute interest and active participation to what is said. If they sense that anything and everything may wander across the preacher's mind and tongue, they attend to nothing. The difference between the two types of sermons is the difference between a registered letter and a piece of fourth-class mail "To the Occupant." Unity does for the sermon what a frame does for a picture. The hearer, as with the viewer of a picture, has the edges of his attention gathered up and focused by the clear sense of being personally addressed with a definite expectation of some kind of response.

There are, of course, preachers who discount all arguments for the single-idea sermon with the insistence that the variety of needs in the average congregation can be addressed only by broad themes and multidirectioned messages. If this response is a cover for a lack of rigorous discipline, no answer is necessary. If, however, a minister sincerely holds this view, he needs to reflect on several considerations to the contrary. First, he cannot say everything at once. He will, therefore, have to set priorities and accept judgment upon his silences as well as his sermons. Second, he should preach as though there will be a tomorrow rather than no tomorrow. He will trust that God will give him occasion to speak again. There is some dramatic force in the "If I had but one chance to preach" psychology, but the pastor who tries to preach on a dead-end street will invariably hang crepe. And finally, he may perceive that, in spite of differences of age, culture, education, and social involvement, there are basic problems and needs common to us all. To deal specifically with one of those needs is to feed not one sheep but many. To say one thing each Sunday for fifty weeks is good medicine; to say fifty things each Sunday is to distribute aspirin in the waiting room.

The singleness of theme that we are considering here is not easily achieved. Any minister who has sought to have a point rather than a parade of points in sermons knows the difficulty. And for the preacher who would take the biblical text seriously, the difficulty seems to be compounded. In fact, it is sermons regarded by those who preach them as biblical that are most commonly lacking in unity. Is there a flaw here in one's use of scripture or is it in the nature of biblical materials that singleness of theme can be achieved only by their violation? A number of observations are called for at this juncture.

In the first place, it may be true that the text has a number of ideas in it. However, thorough exegesis of the passage in its context may reveal that all those ideas are really subordinate to and supportive of a larger overarching issue. Only after this exegetical work is the preacher in a position to decide if this larger issue is of such dimension and importance to require treatment in more than one sermon. It may be that the selected text is too large and has within it two or more now discernible pericopes. Too much at once, as well as too little, may result in a deformation of a writer's meaning. Only careful study in each case enables one to make proper judgment of this matter.

Second, the desire to be thorough in treating a text often leads the preacher to move around within the text, with the result that the apparent thoroughness sacrifices both unity and clarity. This temptation to touch all the bases is especially keen in narrative texts that present a number of characters. For example, the parable of the prodigal son can be scrambled into ineffective confusion by letting the father and the two sons be "the three points" from which applications and lessons are drawn. Or the dramatic story of the healing of the blind man in John 9 offers a real trap here. Unless one takes time to hear the point of the story and make that point the governing consideration, every one of the characters may receive separate, brief treatment as a launching pad for "a lesson for us today."

Third, and in this same vein, there are two forms of seduction in a homiletical use of scripture to which one may fall victim. One is the seduction of the concordance. Suppose the preacher checks a concordance for all the references in which the subject, or at least a key word in the subject, occurs. If the list is considerable, she may feel that a truly biblical sermon would be the use of all these references with a few comments on each passage. And, regretfully, some parishioners will accept this parade of verses as biblical preaching. The preacher herself should know better. The unity is only apparent, not real. The concordance has led her to mistake common occurrences of certain words for common subject matter. And the various documents, themes, and purposes of the biblical writers have been leveled in a near word-magic use of the Bible that violates both spirit and letter of all scripture. Concordances have legitimate functions, but providing sermon outlines is not one of them.

The other form of seduction is that of the easy text. As all Bible readers know, some passages seem to contain prepared and packaged outlines, and sermon-hungry, point-conscious preachers rush upon these as upon oases in a parched desert. How many have come upon John 14:6, "I am the way, and the truth, and the life," and felt they were halfway home in sermon preparation! Unity and structure seem built into the text. This same gift of an instant sermon seems to be offered by Ephesians 3:18, "power to comprehend, with all the saints, what is the breadth and length and height and depth." Who could resist this four-point outline, free for the taking?

The fact is, all should resist every temptation that promises a sermon without struggle, study, appropriation, and decision, even if that temptation is presented by the Bible itself. Whoever allows himself to be so seduced finds that he does not have a sermon, but three or four sermonettes, each related to the others as pegs in a board. In the delivery, transitions are awkward and unity is nonexistent. Exegesis of the two passages mentioned as well as others of this type would have made it clear that no one of the apparent points nor the sum of all of them constitutes the point of the text. It may be that the preacher will find the apparent points of some structural value later on in preparation, but only after his study has led him to *the point* the author sought to make. No preacher has the right to look for points until he has the point. And even then, if unity and movement hold deserved priority, he will not think in terms of points at all, but of transitions, turns in the road, or of signs offering direction toward the destination. Suggestions in this regard will be given in the discussion of structure in the final chapter.

All this has been to say again that unity is difficult to achieve but irreplaceable if the sermon is to move. It is a mistake to assume that text or title or outline provides this unity for the sermon. The desired unity has been gained when the preacher can state the central germinal idea in one simple affirmative sentence.

Careful examination will reveal that most sermons, rather than possessing unity, fall clearly into two parts, regardless of the number of divisions the outline may contain. This is assuming that the sermons make some effort to take seriously the scripture and tradition. This broken unity mirrors the polar nature of the preaching task and testifies to the tension experienced by the person who preaches. Part of the sermon, often the earlier material, is oriented toward the past, scripture and tradition, and represents the minister's effort to share the fruit of research. The other part of the sermon, usually the later material, is oriented toward the present, the congregation, and represents the minister's effort to be relevant and prophetic. There is often a great distance between that past and that present, and the negotiation of that distance is the preacher's hermeneutical task. The task is a difficult one, as the whole history of biblical interpretation reveals, and full of agony for the minister who would internalize the tension that exists inevitably where honesty toward the past and responsibility toward the present are twin motives. But blessed is the preacher who chooses to live with this tension rather than accept the easy unity that costs the release of one of the poles, sacrificing history for modernity or sacrificing the present congregation in adoration of the past. Perhaps it would be helpful to reflect on this tension built into the preaching task, not that such reflection will resolve it, but by understanding its nature, it may be that more preachers will be more bold to preach unified sermons without feeling that yesterday or today has been compromised.

There are a number of ways to view the two poles that threaten the unity of every sermon and yet offer the promise of creativity and the possibility of actually speaking God's Word today. Psychologically, the tension may be said to exist between the tendency toward fixity on one hand and toward flexibility on the other. Some older textbooks in psychology referred to this as the ambivalence between contentment and mastery. Reuel Howe called this ambivalence, in terms of communication, a desire to speak and yet not wanting to; a desire to listen, and yet a fear of doing so.[2] All of us are pulled in both directions, but with more force toward one or the other at different times. Usually the seminary years and the period shortly thereafter are the times when there is greater polarization around flexibility. This is understandable since there is in the academic world an acceleration of questioning and preoccupation with the problematic.[3] The easy rejection of the past during these years is reflected in sermons that, if they possess unity, are unified too quickly and simply about some issue enjoying such currency as to blind one to its historical antecedents. Likewise understandable is the tendency toward fixity among those whom time has made brittle and whose long-buffeted and-trampled ideals are exhausted. The unity of sermons from this quarter is purchased at the price of closing all the unsettling modern freeways of thought and reopening memory lane. The sight of relief and relaxation that settles over the comfortable sanctuary may muffle for the minister the clear announcement of his conscience that he has capitulated.

Liturgically, the polarity of the preaching task may be referred to as order over against spontaneity. Were this tension confined to the matter of differences in traditions and tastes in worship, it could be dismissed as a problem beyond the province of this book. The issue touches preaching, however, not only because some ministers have eliminated either order or spontaneity from their preaching but because they have tended to identify their own preferences with the Holy Spirit. Does order focus and clarify or does it restrict and reduce? Unless one is prepared to accept both answers and be alerted thereby, one's preaching will eventually absolutize either the lectionary or the late news. It is a good practice to discipline one's pulpit with a planned and ordered preaching calendar. Then when an urgent matter arises and insists on interrupting the schedule, that matter will have to earn a place by competing with the subjects for preaching already determined. This test of the strength of any intruding topic is healthy; where there is no planned order of subjects for preaching, the blank page for next Sunday hungrily welcomes every passing issue and invites it into the pulpit. Good preaching always gives the impression of dealing with matters freshly chosen from among competing topics and yet which are mellow from sufficient time in the cellar.

From a pedagogical point of view, preaching embraces the tension between an understanding of itself as a content that is given and yet as an activity that is learned. "Preaching" can be properly defined as both "that which is preached" and "the act of presenting the gospel." The first definition underscores the fact that the message is given to the preacher and to the church. Such a definition reminds the minister that preaching is a gift and moves him into the posture of the grateful recipient. And yet the second definition can be neglected only at the risk of the demise of the pulpit. This understanding of preaching reminds the minister of his task as communicator, as one called to articulate with interest, persuasion, and clarity. The givenness of the content of his communication does not diminish but heightens his obligation to prepare thoroughly, mastering as fully as possible the media by which he will publish the Good News. It is because of the gifts of Brahms and Mozart that the most accomplished pianist is not ashamed to practice scales. Let a preacher focus solely upon the givenness of the content, and we have a gospel that is forever theoretical and potential because it remains locked within inarticulate lips and hidden in confused speech. And yet let him center upon preaching as a learned act, and the measure of his mastery of speech arts will be the measure of his arrogance. Although he cannot resolve them, neither will the minister relinquish either pole of his affirmation, "I worked harder than any of them—though it was not I, but the grace of God" (1 Cor. 15:10).

Historically, the tension within preaching is expressed in the relation between scripture and church. On the one hand, the church not only preceded the New Testament chronologically, but the New Testament was produced by the church, both in its writing and in its selection from among the many available Christian documents. The New Testament is, therefore, the church's book, and she has the right to lay hands on it in bold investigation. On the other hand, the New Testament is the scripture for the church, and before it the church is to sit in obedient submission, open to guidance, discipline, and judgment.

Many Christians have felt this ambivalence in their relation to the scripture. Because this is Word of God, the church is not only invited but urged and obligated to study it. Implied, of course, in this, as in all study, is the bringing to the material of all one's faculties: questioning, discussing, applying all available tools for prying open the mysteries in the ancient documents. In the process, the Bible takes on the physical characteristics of all well-used textbooks. And yet, because this is Word of God, study is inhibited by reverence. A sense of humble respect stays the student's mind and turns aside the critical questions of free investigation. The frequent result is study that really is not study, or reverence that is not really reverence.

Especially does the minister, whose task is to embrace both scripture and church in preaching, experience this ambivalence. Regretfully, she may gain a cheap peace by keeping the desk and the pulpit separated. At the one, she operates as the free investigator of ancient writings; at the other, she recites the sacred phrases as though proper intonations alone would bring healing to the hearers. Eventually, of course, this schizoid pattern loses momentum, the pulpit with its immovable deadlines winning out over the desk, where gathering dust announces the demise of seminary habits.

Blessed is the congregation whose minister offers herself as a frail bridge between church and scripture. Her sermons will possess the unity not of a monologue of the church to the scripture nor of the scripture to the church, but the unity that characterizes all genuine dialogue. It is fabric woven of two distinct and always perceptible threads: The situation addressed precedes the Word of God; the Word of God precedes the situation.[4]

Finally, it may be helpful to conceive the polar nature of the preaching task hermeneutically, for the struggle to achieve unity in sermons that deal seriously with scripture is also the struggle of biblical interpretation. Just as biblical sermons tend to fall into two parts (the meaning of the text and its application), so biblical interpretation has generally divided its task into ascertaining what the text *said*, and what the text *says*. Both steps have seemed necessary where both honesty and relevance were prized, but attainment of unity in the process has been less than satisfying. Preaching that involves the highest level of interest and forcefulness possesses unity, but this unity waits upon a hermeneutical method that negotiates the distance between the congregation and the text without radical discontinuity. This is assuming, of course, that preaching must struggle with the biblical texts, a conviction firmly held here but without the comfort of universal endorsement.

The problem facing the preacher as biblical interpreter has frequently been framed on the "Word of God–word of man" dichotomy. For a number of reasons this has an unsatisfactory way of conceiving the tension, productive of a host of additional problems. First, this concept has led some preachers and many hearers to divide the message easily into two parts, all scripture quotations being Word of God and all interpretation and application being word of man. This not only guarantees for them the purity of God's word, but at the same time it disarms the preacher and assures the church that God will not interrupt with further communiques. Second, this distinction between God's Word and man's word has led some to seek the Holy Grail of exact quotations from the Lord. Once in possession of this slim but one hundred percent red-letter edition, all the portions of the Bible consisting of human interpretation could then be reduced to the status of subcanonical options. Third, the "Word of God–word of man" conceptualization has led to the mystical dismissal of words in a book in favor of the pure immediacy of the Word of God. Or finally, the Divine Word–human word dilemma has in some quarters resolved itself into a compromise: The Word of God is the eternally valid content, and the word of man is the historically conditioned vehicle by which that content is conveyed. This "kernel and husk" theory permits every interpreter to decide what is kernel and what is husk, a permission of such latitude that it quickly defeats itself as a method of interpretation.

All this is to say the preacher who divides the raw materials of the sermon into the two categories of "Word of God" and "word of man" will, all reverence and sincerity notwithstanding, nullify her own effort and fracture her sermon into two neat but equally use-less halves: one with authority and no relevance, the other with relevance and no authority. The reason is that the preacher has done her work on the basis of

> the fundamental misunderstanding according to which God's Word is so to speak a separate class of word alongside the word spoken between men, which is otherwise the only thing we usually call word. God's Word is here said to be not really word at all in the sense of the

normal, natural, historic word that takes place between men. It is said that, if it would reach man, then it must first be transformed into a human word, translated as it were from God's language into man's language—a process in which, as in every process of translation, we have naturally to reckon with certain foreshortenings and distortions. These shortcomings are then exculpated by means of the idea of accommodation, or the process is interpreted as analogous to the incarnation: As God finally took the highest, or lowest, step of becoming man, so (it is said) God's Word earlier, and in another form of course also later, becomes at least a human word. But this is a conglomeration of dreadful misinterpretations...When the Bible speaks of God's Word, then it means here unreservedly word as word—word that as far as its word-character is concerned is completely normal, let us not hesitate to say: natural, oral word taking place between man and man.[5]

A more fruitful approach to the polarity of the preaching task, set in the hermeneutical frame of reference, is to begin with the understanding that all the words we know are human words. We could not experience nonhuman words and therefore should not try to work with the assumption that God spoke a divine language that was then translated into a particular human language. Given, then, the assumption that words are words, how are the words in scriptures to be approached, as *content* to be traditioned, or as *address* to be heard and shared?

Stating the issue as a sharp either/or question is hardly fair, of course, demanding as it does a simple response to a body of literature that is rich in varieties of forms, moods, and functions. Such a structuring of the question does, however, provide a way of getting into the open the complex issue of interpreting scripture. And as a matter of fact, the history of the church's use of scriptures in preaching and teaching has tended to move in an either/or pattern, there being periods of strong emphasis on the scripture as the body of authoritative tradition, provoking a reaction in favor of an understanding of scripture as address to the hearers.

This can be seen in the shift in accent in biblical interpretation prompted by the work of Karl Barth following World War I. Prior to his initiation of a new approach, the Bible was being approached primarily as a body of content from the Judeo-Christian tradition.

To understand more thoroughly that body of literature, a host of helping disciplines had arisen: historical, literary, form, and textual criticism. And very helpful they were.

The preacher should not look upon these disciplines as otherwise, for the Bible as a collection of ancient documents surely deserves the compliment of objective examination as much as other literature. A refusal to make use of these tools to ascertain the proper text reading, its relation to other literature, and the cultural-historical milieu out of which it arose, is a move toward dishonesty prompted either by a fear of what might be discovered or by an impatience to get a sermon that cannot tarry at books that are not heavy with homiletical fruit.

A problem arose for the church's preaching not because of these methods of biblical study but because of an unlimited confidence in the total adequacy of these methods, eliminating any need to attend to the scriptures for anything other than what these tools were able to dredge up. To discover what a writer *said* to his intended readers is demanded, of course, by honest research, but this discovery alone is inadequate if the Bible is to function as the *scripture* of the church. Needless to say, this ascendancy of historical-literary criticism produced a pulpit that was full of research properly footnoted but that fed the congregation a steady diet of remote yesterdays, hardly digestible even if the nutriments were there.

Karl Barth was dissatisfied with this approach, which understood the task of the biblical interpreter to be fulfilled when he, as a subject, had properly understood the text as an object. His dissatisfaction was that of a preacher, but he was wise enough to know that satisfaction would not come with some new and clever way of approaching the past. Homiletical appropriations of the past through allegory, gnostic flights out of the confines of history, archaizing the present, modernizing the past, reduction of texts to universal principles, and a host of other devices were thrown out as failures to take either past or present seriously enough in the effort to hear the Word of God. The problem lay, rather, in the whole subject-object diagram upon which Bible study took place. If the text wrestles with serious questions and if the reader does also, then the reader's own questions are not extraneous intrusions on a "pure understanding" of the text, but are vitally involved in a proper understanding of the text. The text is not, therefore, to be approached with the arrogance that accompanies the notion that the present is always superior to the past nor with that acquiescence that marks the opposite view. Rather, the reader listens as one engaged in serious conversation about ultimately serious matters. Because the reader may not really be serious, she may come under the judgment of the text and discover that she, not the text, has been the "object" interpreted.[6] In this encounter with the text, the Word of God is not simply the content of the tradition, nor an application of that content to present issues, but rather the Word of God is the address of God to the hearer who sits before the text open to its becoming Word of God. Most importantly, God's Word is *God's Word* to the reader/listener, not a word about God gleaned from the documents.

This all-too-brief statement concerning on the one hand interpretation that sees its task as thoroughly grasping historical content, and, on the other, interpretation that hopefully comes to a hearing of God's Word addressing the interpreter is not intended to lead the reader to a choice and to prejudice him in that choice. On the contrary, this statement is merely to illustrate that he does not have to choose; indeed, he must not choose. Karl Barth did not choose. They err who have regarded him as the champion of anti-intellectual Bible-listening, his commentaries on Romans and Philippians being proof enough. Bringing one's own problems and questions to the text does not replace thorough study; rather, it gives study the proper posture and a compelling reason. The point of our present consideration is simply that the preacher must not, in his longing for unity in his messages and in his whole *modus operandi,* accept the easy victory that comes with either/or. Both approaches to scripture sketched above participate in the struggle to understand not just a text but the will of God and the meaning of being Christian in one's context. This understanding is the goal of interpretation, and this understanding gives unity to the sermon. Unity short of this is premature and more apparent than real.

There have been other ways of framing the issue of the fundamental tension that exists between the views of scripture as content and/or as address. Joseph Sittler has labeled the two poles of the hermeneutical struggle "narrative" and "kerygma," locating the tension within the literature of the New Testament itself.[7] Kerygmatic declarations are found primarily in the writings of Paul and John, where the accent is not on a Jesus of Nazareth enmeshed in historical relativities but on the crucified and risen Christ who now calls us out of death into life. Such declarations can be termed "address." Narrative materials, on the other hand, such as are found in the synoptic gospels, present more of the historical account.

However difficult the grappling with the historical elements within "gospel" records, the presence of the first three gospels in the New Testament testify to the church's recognition of the essentiality of the temporal, historical contingencies within her story of redemption. These narratives can appropriately be called "content."

Amos Wilder has analyzed the content and/or address character of the preacher's message as it is being discussed in recent hermeneutical circles from a different perspective.[8] He has raised the issue of the nature of humans and has asked whether the New Testament when viewed solely as content or solely as address has a message capable of redeeming the whole person. He regards it as an inadequacy of the Bultmannian approach that, in viewing the gospel as address, people are viewed simply as volitional beings, called upon to *decide* and nothing more. Humans, Wilder rightly insists, are also noetic beings who need explanations and meaning, who cannot make a "pure" decision apart from their whole social and cultural context. Social, historical, and psychological factors are not accidental to the person who is addressed and are therefore to be regarded positively in understanding God's action in time and place rather than negatively or at best neutrally and as inconsequential to the decision for or against the addressing Word of God. To be sure, the introduction of historical and cultural content into the gospel message raises the fear of the loss of immediacy and threatens the church with an archaic and history-trapped pulpit. But the alternative raises the charge of reducing the Word of God to a decision at the moment and reducing the person to a "decider," abstracted from a context of meaning that the doctrine of creation so positively asserts.

Is the preacher, then, to regard the gospel as content in response to which he seeks belief? If so, he can do no better than to work through his New Testament in order to arrive at a full summary of the items included in the gospel. The best and most influential study of this type is still C. H. Dodd's *The Apostolic Preaching and Its Development.*[9] Professor Dodd arrives at a digest of the kerygma of the early church after careful analysis of the sources in the New Testament, especially Acts and 1 Corinthians. But if this content is preached, how is the preacher to escape Bultmann's charge that his sermons are history lessons calling for consent, a consent that lacks the courage of faith because it requires the support and legitimization of historical evidence before it will say yes?

Is the preacher, then, to move away from historical considerations in search of the immediacy Bultmann has found in regarding the preaching event itself as the eschatological occurrence, the end-time for the one who hears Christ's address in the sermon with the threat of death or the promise of life? This immediacy, this sense of the eternal significance of the present, is for the preacher more precious than rubies. But how shall she escape Dodd's charge that her sermons are gnostic evaporations of history and departures from the tradition that Paul and others, having received it, were careful to pass along to others?[10]

It was said earlier that unity is essential to movement in preaching, and that movement is the first essential to interest and effective power in preaching. However, it was further pointed out that the principal reason for the breakdown of the unity of the sermons of those who prepare for the pulpit is to be found in the polar nature of the preaching task itself. At no point is this polarity more evident and more difficult to negotiate than in the effort to create sermons that have biblical texts as a primary raw material. The geographical, linguistic, psychological, cosmological, and chronological gulf between the ancient Near East and modern America yawns frighteningly wide. It is small wonder that some preachers turn away in their sermons either from the ancient Near East or from modern America, while others dutifully grant equal time to "Background" and to "Application."

We have come, then, to the unenviable position of having asserted that the absence of serious interpretation of the biblical text endangers the Christian character of the sermon while the presence of such biblical interpretation endangers the movement of the sermon and the unity essential to that movement, both qualities being requisites for maximum effectiveness. Obviously, the next step in our consideration must be in the direction of a use of scripture that is supportive of the thesis regarding inductive movement and yet a use that does not violate the honest exegesis that the text demands as the scripture of the church.

CHAPTER 6

Inductive Movement and the Text

The preacher who is doing his reading these days has been encouraged by the fact that there have been a number of recent attempts "to find a new way through from exegesis to the sermon."[1] That these efforts among biblical scholars, systematic theologians, and practical theologians are taking place has several clear implications. First, the fact that they are only "attempts," and some of them not very helpful to the preacher, is a clear reminder that the use of scripture by the church in evangelism, polemics, and instruction is a most difficult problem. The problem is as old as the church, for there has always been a tradition preserved in sacred texts with all the uses and misuses that accompany scripture. Jesus frequently faced the problem of being charged with flying in the face of scripture. The "you have heard it said—but I say" format in the Sermon on the Mount is not a simple "Old Testament or Jesus" antithesis, but rather a question of what is the proper interpretation of the scriptures. And when Jesus was quizzed about divorce on the basis of Deuteronomy 24:1–4 (Mk. 10:2–9), he subordinated that passage as a concession to hard-heartedness and lifted up the Genesis accounts affirming the indissolubility of the marriage union (Gen. 1:27; 2:24; 5:2) as the expression of God's will. By what hermeneutical principle could Jesus say one text expressed God's will while another did not? His opponents could not stand still for this. Nor was the problem solved for the church when it could support its message not only with Psalms and Second Isaiah but with the "Sayings of the Lord," for these likewise had to be interpreted as texts. For example, Matthew's account of the marriage feast (22:1–14) is quite noticeably an interpreted expansion of the earlier form found in Luke 14:16–24. Joachim Jeremias, in his monumental work on the parables, has pointed out clearly the task of the early church in interpreting the words of Jesus. It is important in studying the parables, for example, to see them in the setting of the church and, if possible, in the setting of Jesus' ministry. The difference in settings is important because the church faced the task of taking the words of Jesus to a particular audience and, presenting them as the word of the Lord in a new situation.[2] It took both wisdom and courage for the church to assume this awesome burden of interpreting, but to have failed to do so out of an overwhelming reverence for quotations from Jesus would have ended the work Jesus began. And this work of interpreting anew is not confined in the New Testament to the words of Jesus. As we will notice later in this chapter, traditions such as that of the Last Supper had to be interpreted anew in contexts that differed from the original setting (1 Cor. 11:23 ff.).

We remind ourselves at this point, then, that the route from text to proclamation is an old and difficult one, not such as should discourage the preacher, but rather, should help her to see that interpretation is not an alien and abusive intrusion upon the scriptures. The problem of honest and relevant interpretation of texts is imbedded within the Bible itself and is not to be looked on as an exercise post-biblical in origin. In fact, most of the New Testament can be viewed as interpretations and reinterpretations of the tradition (note 1 Cor. 15:1ff. as one statement of it) in the light of new situations faced on the mission fields of a vigorous and growing church.

We dwell on this point because a real prophetic pulpit today waits on the release of the minister from a shackling hypercaution about interpreting the scriptures as the word of the Lord to our situation. Until this release is effected, the prophetic voices will seem to be those that impatiently cast aside scripture and tradition and speak a new word. The shades of Marcionism move lively again across the pulpit when the church, for reasons probably sincere and rooted in a theology of the Word, is unwilling to take up the task of interpreting scripture for specific contemporary settings. And there would hardly be any clearer go-ahead signal than the recognition that the New Testament itself arose out of the continual interpretation of the gospel for new situations. New interpretations are necessary because the new context of the hearer has to be addressed. The use of Mark by Matthew and Luke represents dimensions of this interpretation process. Or again, 1 Pet. 1:3—4:11 probably had its original setting in a baptismal service, but in the New Testament document before us the baptismal message is interpreted for those who have already been baptized and for those responsible for their care.[3] Without this continuing interpretation and reinterpretation, the text of the gospel would be brief, old, dead, and under glass protecting it from the soiling hands of tourists.

Very likely in the early church those designated as prophets were engaged in this translation of what Jesus *said* into what the Lord *says* to the church in the new situation. They did their work in a church conscious of and open to the Holy Spirit, and yet a church also aware of the risk involved in speaking for the Lord. The Spirit reminds of what Jesus *said* but also leads through that door left open by the words, "I still have many things to say to you, but you cannot bear them now. When the Spirit of truth comes, he will guide you into all the truth" (Jn. 16:12–13). A timid spirit repeats what has been said and feels secure in the continuity; a brash spirit comes up with the new and revels in the discontinuity. But the church needs in each new context the prophetic spirit.

A second implication of the new attempts to move from exegesis to sermon is a recognition of the inadequacy of older attempts. When reading the history of interpretation of scripture, one is permitted to smile but not to laugh at allegory, symbolism, typology, and levels of meaning, for these were sincere efforts to hold the scripture as scripture while insisting that the congregation deserved some relevant word for its own situation. Perhaps equally sincere but no more worthy of the popularity they enjoy are the exegetical methods common today: selection, elimination, reduction to general truths, modernizing biblical characters through popular jargon, or archaizing the present by calling on congregations to "go back to old Jericho for a few minutes this morning." The preacher is not Moses or Paul, and the people before him are not Israelites or Corinthians. To pretend such for homiletical purposes has about as much net gain as is enjoyed by the young man who unconsciously addresses his date as Linda when her name is Judy. Of course, it is far easier to lament the inadequacies of former or current exegetical methods than it is to suggest a better one. All serious preachers are bound by the fear that, in the responsible transaction of changing coinage, there may be a reduction of value.[4]

A third implication of the effort to find a new route from text to sermon is the understanding that exegesis has its natural and proper fulfillment in proclamation. Preaching is not an appendix, an unscientific postscript, or an application totally independent of exegesis itself. The texts originated as sermonic materials, and "proclamation that has taken place is to become proclamation that takes place."[5] That which came to expression in the text must now come to expression anew in the sermon. Since exegesis involves putting the text into the speech of the exegete, the message character of exegesis does not just appear later in the sermon but is intrinsic to the very nature of exegesis.[6] Therefore, the exegete who denies interest in preaching may simply be wishing to distinguish herself from a body of unscholarly clerics, but if her disinterest is fundamental to her methodology, then her exegesis is a barren fig tree.

On the other hand, and this is a fourth implication of the attempts to move from text to sermon, exegesis and preaching are not wholly identical. While exegesis and proclamation permit only relative separation from each other, still the degree of that distinction must be preserved for the health of both. The use of a text *as a text* implies a great deal of effort to understand it as a past proclamation. Every text demands honest historical interpretation. But the fact that it is a text *of scripture* in the church's *proclamation* means that a historical interpretation of a sermon of the past is incomplete. The sermon is not in this sense, then, an exposition of the text but a proclamation of that which the text proclaimed.

This essay is concerned with this route from exegesis to sermon. In the previous chapter a general charge was made against preaching to the effect that sermons that kept exegesis and preaching clearly separate were lacking in unity and movement, while sermons that achieved these by relinquishing either the text or the congregation were irresponsible. Is there another alternative? Two suggestions may help us move in another direction.

In the first place, the route from exegesis to preaching is made unnecessarily difficult in traditional practice by a radical reversal of the mental processes in the transition from the study of the text to the structuring of the sermon itself. If we keep the image of the whole process as a route, the first stage (exegesis) is like ascending a hill while the second (sermonizing) is like the descent on the other side. This shift in motion is keenly felt by the preacher, either as a sense of pleasure in only half of the trip (which half depending upon his inclination toward desk or pulpit) or an ill-defined sense of guilt because his congregation is taken only on the second half of the trip. The shift consists of a transition from inductive to deductive movement of thought. Exegesis is inductive if it is healthy and honest. The particulars of the text—its words, phrases, categories, characters, literary forms, context, writer, readers, date, place—each separately and all together demand attention and contribute to the student's conclusion about the meaning of the passage. If exegesis has to labor under the burden of providing particular support for a dogmatic conclusion already occupying one's mind, it ceases to be exegesis. Essential to exegesis, both in method and motive power, is the thrill of potential discovery. This anticipation sharpens the faculties and moves the study to a fruitful conclusion with a quality in it of which the student can be proud. In fact, the confidence born of this exercise will later register on the hearers' minds not as arrogance, which is usually born in a poorly hidden sense of inadequacy, but as conviction and as convincing clarity.

But all the minister has done thus far is inductive, climbing the hill. The joy of the challenge and the anticipation of the peak are dulled by the fact that she did it alone, without the people. They are not to ascend; they must descend, beginning with the summit of the conclusion of his work (his proposition or thesis) and moving down deductively to particular applications of that thesis. The preacher cannot recapture his former enthusiasm as he breaks the theme into points, unless, of course, his image of himself is that of one who passes truth from the summit down to the people. The brief temptation to recreate in the pulpit his own process of discovering is warded off by the clear recollection of seminary warnings that the minister not take his desk into the pulpit. What, then, is he to do? If he is a good preacher, he refuses to be dull. And so between the three or four "points" that mark the dull deductive trail he plants humor, anecdotes, illustrations, poetry, or perhaps enlivening hints of heresy and threats of butchering sacred cows. But the perceptive preacher knows instinctively that something is wrong with his sermon: not its exegetical support, not its careful preparation, not its relevance; it is the movement that is wrong.

Why not re-create with the congregation the inductive experience of coming to an understanding of the message of the text? For obvious reasons it would not, of course, be an exact re-creation. Technical details pursued through books could not be similarly pursued in an oral presentation, but the minister might be surprised at the mental ability of the people to chase an idea through paradoxes, dilemmas, myths, history, and dramatic narratives if the movement of the chase corresponds to the way they think through the issues of daily life. What people resist in preaching, while courteously calling the sermons "too deep" or "over their heads," is that movement of thought that asks at the outset the acceptance of a conclusion that the minister reached privately in the study or received by some special revelation. Too long have sermons proceeded by that special logic that presupposes that, unlike the marketplace, office, and classroom, "in church everything is possible. There the absolutely incomprehensible becomes as self-evident as a fairy in a fairytale."[7]

It is also true that preaching that re-creates the experience of arriving at a conclusion would for the minister differ from her own study in all the ways that private experiences differ from those shared with others and in all the ways that people differ from books. The speaker herself can expect to make new discoveries in the process of sharing, not simply because of some mysterious "inspiration of the audience" but because communication is fundamental to clear thinking, opening and releasing maximum powers of mind and heart.

The question was asked earlier: Why not the same inductive process in delivery as in preparation rather than a broken path of private induction and public deduction? The full response to this question brings us to the second suggestion for achieving movement and unity on the route from exegesis to preaching. Bluntly stated, the whole idea of moving from exegesis to preaching is fundamentally erroneous and must be rejected to the extent that it implies an inadequate appraisal of the place of the congregation. "From exegesis to preaching" puts the hearers of the sermon in the position of recipients only; they are merely the destination of the sermon.[8] Such a view of the role of the congregation in genuine biblical preaching lacks the support of history in that the relation of scripture and church is a dialogical one, lacks the support of scripture in that the New Testament clearly demonstrates that the life and needs of the congregations addressed contributed greatly to those products we now call books of the New Testament, and lacks the support of actual practice in that the congregation is in the pastor's mind during, not merely at the close of, exegetical work.

Now perhaps it should be said immediately that this is not a call for exegesis that is mere problem-solving activity (as the inductive preaching of late liberal Protestantism tended to be) nor for client-centered preaching that is an exercise in self-analysis and smothering subjectivism occasionally embroidered with scripture verses. It is, however, a call for a program of biblical study and biblical preaching that is more realistic and more responsible as far as the bearing of the congregation's situation upon understanding the message of the text is concerned. Let us see in more detail what this means.

First, the fear of interpreting scripture by and for a congregation as though it were a case of laying soiling human hands upon the Divine or pouring water into the pure wine must be dispelled. If this fear is born of some near-idolatrous view of the text itself, then historical criticism, whatever its faults, helps to release one from this fear. Historical criticism has brought the general acknowledgment of the historical contingency and relativity of every expression of the Word. It can be safely studied in the confidence that even among toppling preconceptions and misconceptions the benefits harvested for thoughtful discipleship will far exceed the sentimental value of the former reverential hesitation. Or perhaps the fear proceeds from a secondhand Calvinism that has darkened the air with gloomy reminders that "we are only human." If so, reading either Testament will bring relief. The stories of creation and of incarnation not only invite everyone to grapple with the Word of God; they charge one to do so.

Second, our membership in the church must be accepted. This is no difficulty if one thinks of a local congregation, nor is it any more painful to affirm membership in a particular denomination or combination of denominations. It is quite another matter, however, to accept membership in the church historic, for this means sharing in the church that witnesses in the New Testament and to which the New Testament witnesses. As was discussed in the preceding chapter concerning church-scripture dialogue, this means being responsible *to* and being responsible *for* the scriptures. It is easier to be cushioned from that responsibility by the intervening centuries, reverting to the "We" and "They" dichotomy that in all areas of life comforts "We" when "They" are in trouble. Belonging to the historic church also means participating in and witnessing to God's continuing activity and revelation rather than locating the time of God in the distant past or future. The congregation finds it simpler and less troublesome to believe the things God *did* as recorded by those few writers who survived the babel of conflicting proclamations of God's Word and achieved canonicity than to venture some faith decision amid differing announcements of what God *is doing* in our time. The preacher also finds it easier homiletics not to risk identifying God's will with or against any current issue, but rather to locate the kingdom of God in an ideal past or an ideal future and then regularly to chastise the people for being born too late or too soon.

Third, it follows that more realistic and responsible biblical preaching means bearing the awesome burden of interpreting scripture *for the congregation to which one preaches.* This does not mean that it is the preacher's responsibility to hand down a more or less authoritative interpretation for them, but as pastor-preacher he will lead them into the experience of hearing the message of scripture *for their situations.* This calls for real courage, courage that moves ahead even while dreadfully conscious of the pitfalls of eisegesis and the thousand chances to be proven wrong by history.

In fact, this courage is rare among preachers, replaced in some by an apparent courage and in others by a reasonable cowardice that passes for humble obedience. Apparent courage translates scripture for sermonic use into the popular jargon and idiom of the day. This seems to bring the Word into our time and make the Bible come alive in our language, but the question is, has the word of promise and of judgment, of gracious offer and of crisis for the world, come through forcefully in this translation, or has the preacher simply been cleverly interesting? Reasonable cowardice that passes for obedience is seen in the practice of quoting the words of the text without translation or interpretation with that humble smile found only on the lips of servants who are delighted that messengers bear no responsibility for the contents or effects of the messages they deliver. Or if an interpretation is given (and it always is, in the very act of selecting this text, in the uses of the voice, mood, etc.), it is identified so completely with the original text that the preacher may safely comment, "If the sermon this morning makes you angry, I am sorry, but remember that I am only bringing you His Word, not mine." After all, should not the one commanding rather than the one executing an order bear the responsibility? So it is that the limitation of conformity to duty permits some ministers a complete freedom from responsibility![9] By this logic the grossest evils have been committed by people who felt no responsibility for what they did because they acted in duty-bound conformity to "the will of God." This fiction can survive even in sincere hearts. The fact is, of course, that every disciple is responsible for how he hears and responds to Christ, and the preacher who proclaims her own hearing in the hearing of others is doubly responsible.

To be sure, the fear of eisegesis is very real, and it often drives a preacher who takes the text seriously to a kind of objective distance from the text as a safeguard against this error. While this caution against an exegesis "colored" by the existential situation is understandable, it is nevertheless true that the present situation adds something other than "color." Sensitivity to the concrete issues of one's own time increases sensitivity to the issues of the text, contributing positively to the understanding of the passage of scripture.

This fact leads to the fourth statement in explanation of the expression of "realistic and responsible biblical preaching": The text is to be studied and shared not in dialogue with "the human situation" in general but with the issues facing the particular congregation participating in the sermon experience. The familiar statement of Hermann Diem, "The congregation is born in preaching," is also true in reverse: "Preaching is born in the congregation."[10] One has only to listen to sermons prepared for a homiletics class with no congregation in view to realize how vital to preaching is the concrete situation. A line fastened at one end in the text but extended into the empty air at the other hardly constitutes an experience of the Word of God.

The matter to be underscored here is the concrete situation of the particular congregation addressed. It is not enough to use the expression "existential involvement" several times in the sermon. Rudolf Bultmann's program of existential interpretation of scripture has rendered real service to the sermon, but Bultmann has not done every pastor's homework. If the program of Bultmann is not carried to the concrete existence of a particular congregation, we are left with a universally applicable interpretation of scripture in terms of "the human situation." Left at this point, the existentialist approach is properly scored for giving us only a generalized *anthropos*, a skeleton of human nature that remains unhistorical as long as it is not specific and concrete.[11] And to the extent that the "New Hermeneutic" does not exhibit sensitivity to the ethical issues of our time in its listening to the Word of God—to that extent it also comes under the same indictment.[12] The whole fabric of the social and cultural life of a person or congregation contributes to the understanding brought to the sermon and is involved in the meaning of salvation that the sermon brings. It is right that preachers be concerned that the Word of God not be hindered, but it is also right that they understand that this hindrance may be caused not only by the mishandling of a text of scripture but by a misreading of the situation of the congregation. Taking the congregation out of context is as much a violation of the Word of God as taking the scripture out of context.

This means, then, that the sermon grows out of the dialogue between a particular passage (not a general and meaningless reference to what "the Bible says") and a particular congregation (not "the human situation"). What comes to fruition is not just a truth but the truth for this community.[13] A sermon so understood would not be the same for different congregations. The one who preaches the same regardless of who comes to hear would probably preach the same regardless of whether anyone came to hear, and the preacher may very well soon have that opportunity. To change one of the partners in a dialogue with no change in the content of the conversation is to admit to a monologue.

A fifth and final statement in elaboration of the idea of realistic and responsible biblical preaching concerns the matter of language. Responsible biblical preaching is not repetition of the words of the text but a new expression of the message of the text in language indigenous to the situation addressed. Two characteristics of the New Testament establish this point. First, there is the presence on every page of the words, categories, myths, images, and technical terminology of the social, cultural, religious, and scientific life of the communities addressed. The early missionaries used these expressions in preaching because they were used every day, and they had to run the risk of being misunderstood in order to be understood. They had no pure, disembodied word to share. Second, there is the immense variety in the affirmations of the gospels, variations dictated by concrete situations. What was the gospel for those living in fear of demons, principalities, and powers? for those who held mortality to be humanity's chief burden? for those married to unbelievers? for those whose livelihood was related to the idol business? for slaves? for employers? What we have in the New Testament are proclamations to concrete situations with the gospel as the text in each case. The text was not just repeated; it was interpreted, translated, proclaimed. An excellent illustration is to be found in 1 Corinthians 11, where Paul's text is the tradition ("The Lord Jesus, on the night in which he was betrayed, took bread…").[14] His text, translated and proclaimed for the Corinthian situation, stands now as our text for proclamation to the situation of the present hearers, a situation that will, in dialogue with the text, create a new speaking and hearing of the gospel. It is a comfort to those who fear something is lost in translation to imagine how much more would be lost if there were no translation. And if the language indigenous to the congregation's life seems unworthy of such a lofty task, it should be recalled that "Jesus…particularly in his parables, exalted everyday life as the 'stuff' of the revelatory event."[15]

This understanding of biblical preaching allows us to pause here in order to sweep aside two issues, one practical and one dogmatic, which should now cease to be issues. The practical question, long discussed by homileticians, has to do with whether one begins with the text or with the people in sermon preparation. This is an important question if the sermon is viewed as a one-way trip from one to the other. However, in the movement here recommended, the experience is not of a trip from text to people or from people to text but, as we have been discussing, actively involves both. It might be helpful to think of it as analogous to the massive dialectic between the existential and the ontological in Martin Heidegger's "hermeneutical circle." His analysis calls first for looking at human existence, then looking at it anew in the light of an understanding of Being as the context for existence, and then correcting and enlarging in view of that context the initial understanding of humanity's existence. Substitute "congregation" and "scriptures" for "existence" and "Being," and the dialogical involvement of each in the other can be seen. Understanding the movement as dialogical should help the preacher avoid, on the one hand, making her congregation mere passive recipients of the text, and on the other, forcing the text to serve up answers to the questions of the congregation. If the matter were to be pressed further by a rejoinder to the effect that even in dialogue one partner speaks first, then the response has to be "the congregation." Very likely most of those who, in fear of a utilitarian captivity of the text, insist on beginning always with the scripture only *think* they are beginning with the text. Every pastor knows that, even with carefully guarded study hours behind locked doors, the people stand around her desk and whisper, "Remember me." They are not intruders; it was in order to be with them that she locked the door.

The dogmatic question that this understanding of preaching regards as no longer real concerns the relation of the Word of God to scripture. Gerhard Ebeling has clearly expressed the inadequacy of the traditional framing of the issue.

> The criticism usually made of the Orthodox doctrine is, that it identifies scripture and the Word of God without distinction. And the correction then made is to say instead of "Scripture is the Word of God" something like, "Scripture contains or witnesses to the Word of God." In other words, to refer to a factor distinct from scripture which has to be sought within or behind it. There is no doubt some truth in that. Yet the decisive shortcoming of the Orthodox position lies in the fact that holy scripture is spoken of as the Word of God without any eye to the proclamation, and thus without expression being given also to the future to which holy scripture points forward as its own future.[16]

In other words, to say the scripture *is* the Word of God or that scripture *contains* the Word of God is to identify the Word of God too completely with only one partner in the dialogue. Word, whether it be of God or of humanity is properly understood as communication, and it is rather meaningless to discuss word in terms of *one* person. Equally meaningless is a discussion of Word of God fixed at one pole, the Bible, apart from the other, the church. Just as sound is vibrations received, so word is a spoken-heard phenomenon. The Word of God, if it is to be located, is to be located in movement, in conversation, in communication between scripture and church. In the absence of that communication, definitions of the Word of God that say "Lo, here!" and "Lo, there!" have to do only with potentiality, not actuality. And this is affirmed in full awareness that there is a strong tradition of preaching that consistently refuses to embrace any position that implies that the Word of God is contingent, modified in any way by the situation of the congregation, or that it moves in any direction other than downward.[17]

Having said all this about biblical preaching that moves inductively, how is the preacher to approach the text as he prepares for his message? First, let it be the text itself that he first confronts, not dictionaries and commentaries about the text. There will be a time for these, but not too soon. It is difficult to get the congregation and the text in conversation if half a dozen experts are already at the table. Not only the congregation but the text falls silent in such circumstances.

Second, let the engagement with the text be a lively one, with real questions being asked. When the text speaks of turning the other cheek, giving away the coat, not looking with lust, being concerned only for today's needs, bearing crosses, loving enemies, tombs opening, demons going into pigs, Jesus ascending into heaven, or the earth dissolving in a great conflagration, what are the immediate human questions? Ministers often are too hasty to reduce all questions into harmlessness with the "Of course, we know this doesn't mean…" type of comment. There is no need to protect the Bible and the people from each other. Let all faculties of mind and heart be free to apprehend and comprehend. Often a text will open up and begin to talk if it has to defend itself against another text. For example, let Paul's frequent admonition to grow up answer Jesus' call to become as little children. Or conversation may be stimulated by asking if there is any truth in the opposite of the affirmation in the text. For example, Paul said, "All things are yours." Is it also true that "nothing is yours"? Oversimplifications, hasty conclusions, obvious half-truths, and one-dimensional moralizing can often be avoided in this way.

Third, listen carefully to the text. This is very difficult to do for a number of reasons, many of which pertain to listening in general. Listening means receiving, and receiving calls for a posture awkward and painful for all except the most humble. It is not only more blessed to give than to receive; it is also much easier. Listening is further hindered by the search for a sermon, a search that can easily dictate to the text what to say, or at least alter the mood of the text. An impatience for a sermon quite often fixes the minister in the mood for exhortations and imperatives, causing her to see them where they do not exist. For instance, "Blessed are the pure in heart" is an affirmation, not a command, but how many times do the great affirmations of the scriptures come out as imperatives in the pulpit. "We must be pure in heart" is a statement entirely different from the text. Changing the mood, even if the same words are kept, is as much a misquoting as a change of the words.

Listening is also hindered by the fact that our culture is saturated with "almost Bible" that continues to pass for scripture.

The minister has breathed this same air and has been affected. Some of this floating material arose from interpretations that gradually moved from the margin of opinion into a textual certainty even though not in the text, such as Jesus' ministering for three years or, while on the cross, committing his mother into the care of the Apostle John. A different type of this hindrance to careful listening to a particular text exists in the oral tradition of a harmonized New Testament. For instance, the concept of twelve apostles, basic to the New Israel, is very significant in Luke-Acts, but in the average Christian mind, it is assumed to be an idea of equal clarity and importance throughout the New Testament. Or again, that Christ died as an atonement for sin is often referred to as "the New Testament teaching" with no consideration of significantly different interpretations of the cross in Acts and the gospel of John. Similarly, such categories as preexistence, or eschatological motifs, or interpretations of the resurrection are generally credited to the whole New Testament in a homogenized view, when what we actually have is a shelf of twenty-seven different works. Study of the gospels, in particular, suffers from such harmonizing, or from the predominance of one of the gospels in the mind of the church to such an extent that the other three are virtually unknown. So familiar is Matthew's account of the confession of Simon Peter at Caesarea Philippi that a use of Mark's account, "You are the Christ," would strike the congregation as a deliberate or careless omission of part of the text. And Christ's response to that confession according to Mark and Luke is so overshadowed by Matthew's account that the minister's use of Mark or Luke would in some quarters confirm suspicions of his heresy. And of course, most congregations take it as unanimous in the New Testament that Mary and Joseph lived in Nazareth before Jesus was born (contra Matthew), that there was at Jesus' baptism a public announcement from heaven as to his divinity (contra Mark and Luke), that Jesus was rejected in his home town because he was a familiar local figure (contra Luke), that Peter was the foremost apostle (contra John), and that Judas hanged himself (contra Luke, in Acts).

All this is not to deny the governing theme of the New Testament that gives it unity, namely, God's redeeming act in Jesus Christ, nor to accent to the point of exaggeration the variety of responses to that act, simply because general themes from the New Testament have flooded our minds since childhood and erased the message of specific texts. Serious study of a single text has to work against the obstacle of an assumed knowledge of the whole. Even familiar texts, which many ministers avoid in sermons simply for that reason, are often not really understood. John 3:16, probably the most familiar, is very commonly linked to the cross as the act of God's giving his Son, when this is not at all John's understanding of God's giving his Son. A preacher would not only render a real instructional service but would have a most satisfying experience in the pulpit if she shared the unfamiliar gospel imbedded in familiar texts. But let her beware of clever and shocking notions; the texts themselves will sustain interest if she will listen to them carefully and then share what is heard. And all temptations to chastise the people for not really knowing the Bible will be squelched by the discoveries the minister himself makes in passages he thought he knew thoroughly.

A fourth guideline for dealing with the text in sermon preparation continues the idea of hearing the text, but it would more properly be called "overhearing" rather than hearing. It is possible that one may approach a text so eager to hear what it is saying that a sermon may be forced out of it prematurely. Pressing the text to speak here and now may foreclose the possibility of hearing what the writer of the text intended to say to the readers. And honesty demands the author be allowed to say what he intended to say. This puts the preacher in the position of one overhearing what Mark or Paul or John was saying to the readers.

Overhearing is an exercise most helpful in sermon preparation. It serves truth by keeping enough distance to preserve objectivity. It leaves the text free of personal interruptions so that it can speak. It leaves one free to listen because, since she is overhearing and therefore not directly addressed, there is no feeling of being threatened, challenged, exhorted by the message of the text. Being thus free, she finds herself being drawn in, identifying, empathizing, and really hearing what is being said. It is the experience of being at the theater: No character on stage directly addresses the audience; the characters address one another. The audience is overhearing, but as the play progresses, the audience begins to identify, to reflect, to feel, to hear.

The experience of overhearing as prelude to hearing is made possible by the historical reconstruction of the relationships and conditions that prevailed between writer and reader of the text. Who is saying what to whom and for what reasons?

If this historical reconstruction sounds like hard work, it is. It is not so difficult if one knows both writer and reader, as in the case of Paul to the Christians in Corinth, Greece. It is more difficult if, as in the case of some biblical documents, one can identify the writer but not the reader or the reader but not the writer. And of course, most difficult is the effort to reconstruct a relationship and a message when both writer and reader are anonymous. Such is the case with the gospels. But it is not impossible, because special accents, recurring themes, repeated warnings or promises help the student of a biblical document to recover with some confidence the occasion and intent. Such historical reconstruction—this overhearing the polemics, the worship, the proclamation, the ethical struggle of the early church—confirms the familiar truth that a knowledge of the entire document is necessarily prior to a knowledge of any particular text within that document. To understand the general purpose and theology of Mark or Galatians or First Peter enables one to preach with confidence on any text within those books.

Nor should the minister look upon this historical reconstruction as so much dull and heavy spadework, sweaty loyalty to old seminary disciplines. In the course of this study, lights come on, insights burst upon the mind, and the imagination is released. Consider this analogy from personal experience. Some time ago I was a luncheon guest in the home of a member of the church where I had been a pulpit guest that same day. My hostess produced an old typewritten sermon that, I was to learn, had been preached by her father thirty years ago. She asked what I thought of the sermon, and after a few complimentary things about its construction, I told her frankly that I personally did not get much from it. She then explained that in 1944 her father, a pastor in the town, was concerned for the spiritual welfare of the German POWs held in a compound near the town.

Gaining permission and securing a translator, he preached, with much uncertainty but with genuine love, this sermon. After her story I asked to read the sermon again. With the historical reconstruction, it was a new and moving sermon. Now able to *overhear* it in its original setting, I was able to *hear* it afresh.

Briefly, a fifth word about the preacher's handling of the biblical text: Once a text is selected, a decision needs to be made as to where one stands in the text. If the text is from Paul to the Thessalonians, does one stand with Paul and address the congregation as the Thessalonians, or does one stand among the Thessalonians and listen to Paul? It makes a whale of a difference in content and mood and delivery. If the text deals with a dispute between Jesus and the

Pharisees, does the minister assume the role of Jesus and lay it on the Pharisees (the congregation), or stand with the Pharisees and listen to Jesus? Unless the decision is made, it is likely that by natural gravitation the minister will be Paul, or Jesus, or the father in the story of the prodigal, or the master talking to the servants, or some other favored character in the biblical scripts.

If the minister discovers that he has in his sermons assumed all the favored roles, always the speaker and not the listener, it would be healthy to stand elsewhere now and then. Stand as a Pharisee and listen to Jesus' defense of his disciples plucking grain on the Sabbath (Mark 2:23ff.) or of his association with publicans and sinners (Mark 2:15ff.). It does not take long to sense the threat and offense the Pharisees experienced. As a result, not only will they be represented more fairly and sympathetically but Jesus will be heard with a new appreciation of the risk and courage it takes to follow him. Be the older brother in the story of the prodigal and listen with his ears to the music and dancing. Are you *really* in favor of parties for prodigals? Stand between the disciples and the woman who "wasted" the jar of perfume worth sixty dollars (Mark 14:3ff.) and listen to both sides of the argument between aesthetics and practicality. Sit in the boat as Zebedee with a lapful of fishing nets and watch your two sons leave you with the work while they walk off after an itinerant preacher (Mark 1:19–20). Are you happy and proud?

Understand, this is not a game, a device for some new sermons on old texts. This issue has to do with one's approach to any text. Does one preach *on* a text or get *into* it, listen to it, and share what is heard? The issue is whether or not we who preach have heard the Word. Anyone who has been thrilled, frightened, moved, paralyzed, honored, humbled, and inescapably addressed by His simple call, "Follow me," has the basic raw material for a sermon.

A sixth and final suggestion for approaching the text in anticipation of preaching has to do with attitude toward the minister's own study. It is commonly known that many pastors spend more time lamenting lack of study time than in actual study. Of course, the pastor is busy, or should be, and the fact that she is no longer in the seminary library impresses itself early upon her. No suggestions will be made here about establishing priorities and carving out precious study time. Only this one sentence will be devoted to urging not only the irreplaceable importance of careful study but the need to come clear in one's mind that time in study is, in a vital sense, time spent with all the congregation. They share in what goes on there and will benefit continually from it. The point more pertinent to present purposes is the minister's recognition of the positive value for study of the scripture that there is in the fully engaged ministry, which on the surface seems to stand in the way of that study. The documents of the New Testament arose out of the church in mission, in the task of evangelizing, edifying, correcting, comforting, opposing error, and, in general, witnessing publicly and from house to house. Some writers, of course, carry more than others the sense of urgency, the noise of battle, the heat of debate, the movement of swift feet on the mountains, but they also served who gave themselves to the less exciting tasks of catechism and copying texts. To the extent that the minister gives herself to that same mission in the world, she will harvest a clarity of understanding texts that arise out of that mission. Common purposes and commitments greatly enable communication, and the minister who sits at her desk already weary from the exercise of mission is more open and ready for dialogue with her apostolic predecessors than is the preacher who, guilty and embarrassed, interrupts idle hours to study the text for Sunday.

It is usually the case that the person most given to his mission as minister is also the person who is most conscious of his need for more time in his study. But he is also the person who should be encouraged by the fact that the fullness of ministry prepares him for the most fruitful use of the study time he has. In his case, the conversation between the scripture and the church begins immediately. The immensity of his problems makes him a willing listener to the text; the significance of his task gives him something to say in response.

CHAPTER 7

Inductive Movement
and Structure

Let us suppose that the conversation has taken place between the text and the congregation, in the person of the minister, who not only knows the congregation's situation in the world but who really belongs to that community herself. Let us further suppose that the sessions have been fruitful; the Word of God has been heard. How, specifically, is it to be shared? Or, in the traditional framing of the question, how is the point to be made into points, how many and in what order?

If one were to compare a large section of scripture with a file of sermons based on that section, one of the most noticeable differences between the two would be the striking variety in the literary forms of the one as over against the dull uniformity of the other. The Bible is rich in forms of expression: poetry, saga, historical narrative, proverb, hymn, diary, biography, parable, personal correspondence, drama, myth, dialogue, and gospel, whereas most sermons, which seek to communicate the messages of that treasury of materials, are all in essentially the same form. Why should the multitude of forms and moods within biblical literature and the multitude of needs in the congregation be brought together in one unvarying mold, and that copied from Greek rhetoricians of centuries ago? An unnecessary monotony results, but more profoundly, there is an inner conflict between the content of the sermon and its form. The minister is seriously affected by the conflict. The content calls for singing, but the form is quite prosaic; the message has wings, but the structure is pedestrian. Energy that should be entirely channeled in the delivery is thus dissipated in the battle of the sermon against itself. The hearers may detect the inner contradiction and neatly label the problem: The minister does not have conviction and enthusiasm; his whole life is not caught up in his words; David is trying to fight in Saul's armor.

The importance of an inner harmony between form and content is illustrated in Nathaniel Micklem's *The Labyrinth Revisited*, in which he explains in a brief preface why his philosophic theme should come to the reader in metric shape.

> I wrote this book in careful, plodding prose,
>   Corrected every sentence; all was fit
> For press and public, free from every pose
>   Or literary scandal, every bit
>   Tidy, exact. But when I finished it,
> I felt that in the telling all the bright
> Wonder was flown and quenched my vision's light.[1]

Of course, some ministers have sought to break the monotony of the usual outline, but these refreshing alterations have been so rare that the minister has been self-conscious about the change, and the attention of the congregation has been stolen by the novelty of the sermon. And often these gropings after a new style are no more than tinkering with the introduction and conclusion, or perhaps, after a false diagnosis of the nature of the illness, taking into the content of the sermon large doses of undigested heresies or controversies simply to stir the drowsy listeners. There are, however, more constructive ways of keeping the passengers awake than by putting rocks on the road.

There is much to be said for variety in sermonic forms simply for the sake of granting relief to both speaker and hearers in an occasion that occurs every week. However, the taste for variety should not lead the minister to adopt structures for his material that violate not only the content but also his understanding of what the preaching experience is. *How* one communicates comes across to the hearers as *what* one communicates, and they receive very clear impressions of what the speaker thinks of himself, his text, his sermon, his congregation, and the world. There is no avoiding the fact that the medium is a message, if not *the* message.

In the case of inductive preaching, the structure must be subordinate to movement. In fact, this subordination means that in most cases the structure is not visible to the congregation. Everyone understands, of course, that in pursuit of certain polemic or didactic aims, a preacher might wish that a series of clear statements be lodged in the memory of the hearers. She may, therefore, not only itemize these statements as she develops them, but repeat them in the conclusion. Such occasions are rare, and in the usual ministry, other opportunities are amply provided for instruction and polemics so that the pulpit does not have to be so used. Usually, for the skeleton to be showing, with a sermon as with a person, is a sign of malformation or malnutrition. The movement of the sermon is so vital to its effectiveness that a structure should be provided that facilitates rather than hinders that movement. And it is a clearly experienced fact that "points," announced or otherwise made obvious, interrupt both the unity and the movement of a sermon. Some of the congregation, especially the young people, find the "points" useful for estimating the hour and minute when the terminus can be expected. The process is simple arithmetic: time the first point, multiply that by the number of "points" announced ("I have *three* things to say about this matter this morning"), and one has not only something to anticipate but a fair estimate as to when to expect it. The minister himself experiences the awkward presence of these "points" in his sermon. For example, the transitions from the bottom of a point now thoroughly treated to the top of the next major section are at times so difficult that even the coupling of conjunctions, transitional phrases, and impressive throat-clearings will hardly bridge the gulf. Ministers who write their sermons from an outline often find the structure an obstacle. For this reason, not a few confess to writing the sermon and then outlining what they have written. While such a practice is considered by some practitioners to be a homiletical crime, there is an instinct at work in this procedure that is fundamentally sound simply because it more nearly corresponds to normal communication.

Not only does inductive preaching demand of an outline that it be subordinate to movement; it demands that the outline, however it may look on paper, move from the present experience of the hearers to the point at which the sermon will leave them to their own decisions and conclusion. It bears repeating that a preaching event is a sharing in the Word; a trip, not just a destination; an arriving at a point for drawing conclusions, not the handing over of a conclusion. It is unnatural and unsatisfying to be in a place to which you have not traveled.

Let the preacher, then, first of all know where he and the congregation are going, whether this be in the proper sense a conclusion or whether this be a point at which he stops, leaving each person to draw his own conclusion, as Jesus often did in the parables.[2] Whatever the nature of this destination, it will be the fruit of preparation and lively engagement with the biblical text, it will be clear to the minister, and it will be the beginning point for the sermon preparation proper. He dare not start with the introduction. If he does so, one of two errors will likely be committed. In case his conclusion is not clearly in mind, he will commit all the blunders of a guide who does not know where he is going. If the conclusion *is* well in mind, beginning sermon preparation with the introduction will produce an introduction that has the conclusion in it, destroying all anticipation, and being in fact a brief digest of the whole message.

One begins, therefore, with the terminus. Perhaps a statement of the conclusion could be written at the bottom of a sheet of paper. The question now is, by what route shall we come to this point? Shall it be brief, or will brevity leave some unprepared to assume the responsibility that begins at the end of a sermon? Shall it be slow or fast? The complexity of the matter and the type of listener will determine this. Shall we go with singing and laughter, or are we to tiptoe in hushed reflection? Are we going to battle, to school, to a forum, to a reunion, to a strange city, to work, to rest, or to a new mission? Will all or some or none arrive ready for the trip? Do they want to go? All these questions, and more, are but ways of planning the trip that, on a sheet of paper, will be called a sermon outline. Above everything else, the minister wants all, if possible, to make the complete journey. She wants to sustain anticipation so that, while the trip will not be the same experience for everyone, all will stay to the end. She desires also that it be an experience for the whole person, all faculties being engaged.

Such an image of the sermon does, of course, find somewhat artificial the traditional structuring of a sermon into three appeals: to the mind, to the emotions, to the will. While all these facets of human capacity are involved in inductive preaching, they are involved in the more natural and normal way—that is, together. This psychological pattern is supposedly based on the natural process that salesmen understand to be the ordinary way customers come to the point of making a purchase. But the salesman-customer analogy is totally inadequate to carry the full dimensions of the preaching event. In addition, this trinitarian formula probably fits very few people. Observation and experience indicate many rather normal people place emotion earlier on the agenda, with intellect limping along later, giving reasons for the course already taken. One reason we need the preaching of the gospel is that people are not living by this neat formula. Among the hearers will be many who have felt one way, thought another, and who cannot remember whether their present situation is the result of any clear decision of their own will. This is tragic, of course, and the preacher would have it otherwise, but he is the minister of, the preacher to, these people as they are, and he wants to communicate. The outline is made for man, not man for the outline.

As she ponders the movement of the sermon to achieve the desired experience, the minister would do well to reflect on dramas seen, stories read, conversations shared. What was the nature of the movement that carried the participant along to a complete experience or, at least, to the point of being convinced that he had things yet to do if his life was to be complete? What was the format? In one case, interest in a person or event is assumed, as with the assassination of a president, and the format is simply the narration of the events involved. In another, the reader or observer is brought to interest by the presentation of a series of experiences, the outcome of which is uncertain. In yet another, a flashback is used, opening with some penultimate scene such as a murder trial, and then the events leading to the trial are brought forward by "remembrances." Or perhaps two persons representing entirely different value systems are joined by business contract or marriage bond and the ensuing struggle enlists interest and almost visceral participation. The variety of structures is endless, many of them brilliantly devoted to no loftier aim than to entertain, to make money. Has the minister thought that the loftiness of her theme, the eternal significance of her message, has rendered unnecessary such efforts toward gaining the involvement and participation of the hearers? Should it not rather be the reverse: having such a theme, can she do less than those who screw all their powers to the task of making the evening entertaining?

Perhaps three brief examples of the vital function of movement in the total experience of sharing a message will illuminate what has been said and free us to move on.

It is common knowledge that, despite its wide familiarity, Edgar Allan Poe's *The Raven* continues to grasp the reader and hold him even beyond its last powerful line. Poe has written an essay in which he describes the process of writing a poem.[3] His first composition was the stanza that he thought would be ultimate but that finally became penultimate. Then, Poe says, his task was to create a series of stanzas that would bring his readers to be able to experience that stanza. He realized preparation of mood as well as mind was vital. It was only later, after much careful work, that he came upon the way to begin that experience for his reader, not too suddenly, setting up resistance, and yet without wasting words: "Once upon a midnight dreary, while I pondered..." Every stanza provides an experience of its own, yet quickening anticipation of the next, until the last haunting syllable. Even then, the appetite is not completely satiated nor feeling exhausted. And so it should be; the readers have the right and the responsibility to bring something of their own to the occasion.

Thomas de Quincey, an English writer of the eighteenth century, chose as his principal medium the essay and as his principal subject matter the social, political, and ethical tidbits that were either overworked or tossed aside as of no consequence. De Quincey, however, saw in small matters the major stuff of ordinary life and wished to highlight the fact that, for most of us, life is a number of small incidents or decisions that make or break us. It was, of course, necessary, if he kept his readers with him all the way, to come to his point obliquely. After all, a direct and obvious discussion of what is generally regarded as a trifle is to have one's essay tossed away, unread. Movement into his thesis was vital to the communication of that thesis in such a way that the reader would be engaged by it and hence would ponder it. The following example shows how one man moves with sustained interest and surprising force to a point that, handled otherwise, would have sounded like another dull preachment about "life's little things."

> For, if once a man indulges himself in murder, very soon he comes to think little of robbing; and from robbing he comes next to drinking and Sabbath-breaking, and from that to incivility and procrastination. Once begun upon this downward path, you never know where you are to stop. Many a man has dated his ruin from some murder or other that perhaps he thought little of at the time.[4]

A third example is drawn from the New Testament. In a series of parables, gathered and preserved in Luke 15, Jesus defends his ministry, which had come under heavy fire from those critics who recognized unsavory characters in his circle of disciples. Jesus presents his own work as the joyous recovery of the lost. As there is no tragedy quite like being lost, there is no joy quite like being found. The celebration is too much for one family; friends and neighbors are called in. But while neighbors rejoice, a son and brother in the family most touched by the drama of lost and found is unable to celebrate. To him, a concerned father explains the party in these words: "For this son of mine (v. 24; brothers of yours, v. 32) was dead and is alive again; he was lost and is found". Our present concern is to notice only the arrangement, the movement of ideas. An entirely different story representing another set of values would be expressed if the order were: "This my son was lost, and is found; he was dead, and is alive again." As it is, the listener is brought to sense the abyss of lostness by placing the word *lost* out beyond the word *dead*, and the height of joy in being found by locating *found* beyond *alive*. The order and movement of the phrases say there is that which is worse than death and that which is better than life.

In each of these examples—a poem, an essay, and a parable—movement performs two functions. First, the movement sustains interest and preserves the anticipation necessary not only to hold attention but to prepare the hearer's mood or mind-set to grasp and participate in the central idea when it comes. Second, the movement is integral to content, to what is being said. Change the order of the phrases and ideas and you have a quite different message. There is a content-force in movement that cannot be replaced by increased volume or multiplied words or other common efforts to recover by quantity of sounds what has been lost by improper or ineffective movement of ideas. A sermon is in bad need of repair if the composer of it discovers that the component parts can be switched about with only slight alteration of meaning and hardly any loss of power.

Perhaps this is the time to pause and address the objection that has probably arisen: namely, that this view of preaching calls for more artistic ability than most ministers possess. To be sure, ministers differ in artistic ability and those at both ends of the scale have special problems: at one end, the problem of communicating; at the other, the problem of communicating *the gospel*. Most ministers, however, possess more capacity for artistic expression than they realize. In many cases, traditional instruction in homiletics has not encouraged latent gifts, with the result that the capacity was either not developed, or if it was, it found expression in areas other than preaching the gospel. This may be a result of that common notion of art that identifies it with embroidery and sets it over against truth. If in one's mind art and truth are so juxtaposed that the increase of one means the decrease of the other, art must forfeit the contest for the sake of the gospel. However, in our present consideration, "artistic expression" means simply the careful unfolding of an idea in a way consonant with the content and mood of that idea. In other words, homiletical structures should not be allowed to violate and distort the finer sensibilities that seem naturally to make the adjustments appropriate to the subject matter. If "art" in this sense seems to take a disproportionate amount of time in sermon preparation, it can be safely assumed that this time will diminish as the process of unlearning clears away artificialities that obstruct communication.

From where, then, does a preacher get an outline pattern or structure for an inductive sermon? By this time it should be obvious that there is no single model available as is true with the traditional form of preaching:

Introduction
Body:
I.
    A.
        1.
        2.
II.
Conclusion

One might experiment with the possibility, since the traditional form is deductive, of inverting the structure to make it inductive.

        1.
        2.
    A.
        1.
        2.
    B.
I.

Here, at least, one has the impression of movement up to, rather than down from, a point. However, if the sermon had several points, all the old problems with points would reappear. The preacher might also discover that while his format looked inductive on paper, his own mental habits and patterns of development of ideas were the same as before. It probably is wisest, therefore, to be less concerned about how the sermon looks on the paper and be more attentive to the arrangement of the ideas. Outlining as such has enjoyed too much prominence in the history of preaching and of teaching homiletics, obviously for the reason that a sermon has been viewed as a rational discourse rather than as a community event.

If the minister feels lost at first with a body of ideas without a skeleton, she may adopt the form in which the biblical text is presented.[5] Amos Wilder has written most helpfully of the forms of early Christian rhetoric.[6] Many oral and written forms lay at hand and were employed by the Christian community for communicating the gospel. In addition, modifications or entirely new forms were created because not every mode of discourse is equally congenial to the gospel. It is a very real question whether the later decision to use the forms of Greek logical discourse did not of itself radically affect the nature of the message, the type of audience to which it would appeal, and eventually the constituency of the church. Even if the adoption of Greek rhetorical forms for sermon outlines was a wise choice in the mission to the Hellenistic world, certainly after nineteen centuries the time has arrived for critical review of sermon form as well as content.

If the speech-forms of the Bible were adopted, sermons would be strengthened by the fact that the text would not be forced to fit a new frame. In other words, narrative texts would be shared in narrative sermons, parables in parabolic form, biography in biographical sermons, and similarly in other speech models. However, Wilder properly warns against trite imitation.

> For example, that because Jesus used parables we also should use illustrations from life, or because the New Testament has a place for poetry we also should use it. All this is true. But there is rather the question of what kind of story and what kind of poetry. Nor should we feel ourselves enslaved to biblical models whether in statement, image, or form. But we can learn much from our observations as to the appropriate strategies and vehicles of Christian speech and then adapt these to our own situation.[7]

One reason for a discriminating selection of speech-forms, even from the pages of the Bible, is the radical difference in the speaker-hearer relationship in our time as over against authoritarian societies. Preachers today cannot operate on the assumptions regarding the hearers' view of the speaker that prevailed in prior centuries, when it was generally accepted that authority resided in a few, not the many. And especially is our society different in that the authority figure in most communities is not a clergyman, as it once was, but very likely the scientist, whether or not the community knows one personally. For this reason Wilder's warning needs to be doubly heeded, for all the rich variety that the adoption of biblical speech models would bring to the pulpit.

The very nature of inductive preaching renders it impossible to suggest "the" outline pattern. Unlike the inductive preaching of the 1920s, which imitated the problem-solving pattern of science, here induction embraces a range of human needs, faculties, and experiences beyond problem-answer activity. However, a few suggestions may help those who wish to begin to employ such movement in their preaching. First, it is to be remembered that preaching is *oral* communication, and, as was pointed out earlier, there are great differences between oral and written communication. It is to invite problems, therefore, to devote the major part of preparation to writing outlines and manuscripts and a minor part to preparing to share orally what is written. It is reasonable that one operate as much as possible in preparation as one will operate in delivery. This does not mean "practicing" the finished sermon. This can make the actual preaching a flat and deadly anticlimax. Oral preparation is working at how to *say* it, not how to outline it or write it. A tape recorder can be helpful if one imagines sharing an idea, a story, an argument with a friend. Play back the tape and observe the order of ideas. Better still, by talking through parts of the sermon with someone, the minister himself can sense the flow of his ideas. Again, this is not *after* writing the outline; preparation is not yet that far along.

Second, by playing back a tape, or reflecting on how ideas were shared in conversation, or sitting alone and imagining the preaching event itself, as the sermon unrolls, one can list by words, phrases or brief sentences the ideas in the order of their occurrence. They may be numbered straight down the page but not structured into any outline. The question is, does the material move along, evoking ideas and sustaining anticipation until the end? Is it, in the proper sense of the term, a good story?[8]

Third, look for the transition points, the moments in the telling of it that will be marked by "And yet," "However," "But," "On the other hand," "Beyond this," "And," "Therefore." If we maintain the image of a trip, the transitions mark turns or changes in the direction and in the elevation of the road. There will be slow turns ("however," "and yet"), sharp turns ("but," "on the other hand"), straight stretches ("and"), uphill drives ("moreover," "in addition," "also," "beyond this," "in fact"), and arrivals at the top ("so," "therefore," "now"). If it is observed that the ideas are invariably joined by *and*, the minister should be warned thereby. Any traveler knows that long, straight stretches of road are dangerous because they induce sleep. Beyond the monotony, however, such a level movement of material indicates an oversimplification to the point of unreality. Life does not move along with each new page in the diary beginning "and...and...and so..." If people with such lives sit before the pulpit, now, at least, a new direction is offered. The gospel interrupts the flow of their personal history and says, "But..."

Fourth, underline these transitional phrases or set them slightly to the left, or type them in capitals. They are not "points," of course, but they will function quite well as pegs on which to hang series of ideas, preserving the hard-won flow of material. In the event a fellow minister sees the "outline," however, one should be prepared for comments reflecting surprise, curiosity, and maybe jests about the poverty of thought in "points" entitled "However" and "Yet perhaps."

By looking at these transitional expressions, the preacher can readily see the movement of thought and the format that provides its shape. One can almost feel the progression of thought by such phrases as:

"It seems...but still..."
"Of course...and yet..."
"Both this...and this...yet in a larger sense..."
"Certainly it isn't the case that...however...so perhaps..."
"You have heard it said...but..."

Some sermons will move in a circle, a statement being made, pursued, then stated again, the latter now seeming an entirely different statement from the original. Sometimes the text will not appear until given at the end, the movement to it being adequate preparation for the reception of it. Perhaps a sermon may be a carefully prepared trip to the edge of absurdity, the congregation being led to see the true nature of a prejudice or a selfish charity. The preacher may devote the message to a defense of the indefensible, each stage of the development moving hearers progressively in the opposite direction. She may take a route exactly parallel to the path her community is taking toward ethical compromise or denial of the Christian mission, and yet the minister knows that if she dealt with the issue in a direct and obvious way, heated emotions would hinder clear reflections. The listeners will transfer the sermon to the issue just as Jesus' hearers were able to perceive that he was talking to them.

The point must be clearly understood that these various movements in preaching are not games of hide-and-seek or cat-and-mouse. The sole purpose is to engage the hearer in the pursuit of an issue or an idea so that he will think his own thoughts and experience his own feelings in the presence of Christ and in the light of the gospel. An oblique approach is not the trick of a coward; it is often the powerful vehicle of someone whose primary concern is not to appear every Sunday as Captain Courageous "telling them off," but to communicate with people who after the sermon is over will have to continue thinking their own thoughts, dealing with their own situations and being responsible for their own faith. Some preachers do, of course, think of the gospel as a searchlight, and there is for them an uncontrollable joy in turning that beam down dark streets and watching the sinners run. However, now that most of the sinners have stopped running, the fun is sharply reduced. Why not a method that invites a person to walk again down the street where he lives but this time in the presence of a Third? It may be that he will see his street as never before, his heart burning within him as the Lord is made known to him in the sharing of the Word. He may decide to change that street or to live on it anew, but the point is, *he* will decide because he has been permitted to decide.

It will probably be true that the preacher will discover many of her sermons will have two transition poles rather than the usual three points. This is not because she is trying to be different or that sermons have to be shorter these days. She will often use such a format for the same reason Jesus did. Jesus preached in a society that had, through long association, custom, and familiarity become blind to the message in the scripture they possessed, deaf to the voice of the God they possessed, and unaware of the presence of the kingdom they planned to possess. The culture in which ministers preach today is quite similar, with its Bible belts, praying together to stay together, and easy identification of material gain and the favor of God. In such situations, preaching has to address these easy assumptions and blind familiarities; the text of scripture has to fight its way through the "almost scripture" that is everywhere to be found and passes for biblical support of custom and prejudice. Hence the format "You have heard...but..." of Jesus and the need for a similar structure in our time. It can be done without messianism.

She who preaches inductively will need to be prepared for frequent comments from the congregation to the effect that her sermons seem to be long introductions with a point stated or implied at the end.[9] The minister may interpret this a number of ways. She may reflect critically upon the sermon: is she being too subtle and inconclusive? She may recognize that the congregation is having to adjust its own psyche and ear to hear this preacher who speaks as one who has no authority. She may be mildly pleased that this remark indicates her sermons are interesting and move in a way natural for the listener. She may, however, detect that for which she had hoped: The congregation cannot shake off the finished sermon by shaking the minister's hand. The sermon, not finished yet, lingers beyond the benediction, with conclusions to be reached, decisions made, actions taken, and brothers sought while gifts lie waiting at the altar. Those who had ears heard, and what they heard was the Word of God.

Appendix A
The Sermon Process

It might be helpful to illustrate the process of sermon development and delivery that has been discussed in the preceding pages. This sample is not a finished sermon, but rather is a sketch of the process.

The conception of the sermon. However vague at this point, there has to be the germ. It may spring from a text or from the life situation of the congregation. The place of origin is not important so long as both text and congregation are permitted to respond to each other.

This sermon arose from the reading of a text, Philippians 1:12–18, especially verse 18. It is a surprising and arresting statement: "Christ is proclaimed in every way, whether out of false motives or true; and in that I rejoice." Paul has opponents in the ministry who apparently preach out of strife and divisiveness, and Paul seems to disregard the motive, celebrating the fact that they are preaching. Is Paul really subordinating motive for a greater good—a Christian act? Sounds like a good word for hypocrisy! But then, is it possible that some of us are too concerned about inner feelings, too preoccupied with motives? And yet the other extreme is frightening.

Playing with the idea. Here, open all the faculties, permitting the idea to trigger thoughts, feelings, memories, former ideas, and so on. Be playful, jot down ideas, but forget about order or sequence.

In Philippians 1:18 Paul disappoints us at first. He seems to contradict Jesus' emphasis on the pure heart and all our Christian training to the effect that nothing you do can be right if your reason for doing it is wrong. Did not church people applaud Washington

Gladden for returning to John D. Rockefeller a gift to missions because "the gift without the giver is bare"? And the real force in the voice of the Fourth Tempter in T. S. Eliot's *Murder in the Cathedral* is the offer "to do the right thing for the wrong reason." Basic to our accepted understanding of the Christian life is not only that heart and hand agree (integrity) but that all that the hand does should be from the heart. The order of business is: think it and feel it; then do it. Reverse the order and you have hypocrisy. We have been advised and we have advised: Don't do it unless you sincerely feel it.

Arriving at clarity. We need, then, to turn again to the text. Does Paul really say what he seems to say—that he can celebrate a Christian act that is not from a Christian motive? Here the tools and skills of a contextual and textual analysis are put to work. The preacher begins with the text as would any member of the congregation, asking the immediate and spontaneous questions, as in the paragraph above, but now the responsibility as pastor-teacher-preacher demands exegetical work, careful and honest.

And so Paul *does* say it, but how can he? Is there a flaw in our priority on motive? Has he a word for us here?

Well, on an elementary level, doing something without an adequate or proper inner motive is, regardless of all theories and theologies, necessary. Floors are swept, meals cooked, diapers changed, doors opened, papers graded, classes taught, even sermons preached because some things must be done even when we are not at/about all excited doing them. Waiting for the heart to prompt us would bring the world to a grinding halt.

And it can be a healthy exercise to act first and feel later. The old James-Lange theory in psychology insisted that feeling follows the act. Interest in a book *follows* study. How often we don't really want to, but we do, then we are glad we did. Surely it isn't hypocrisy in a bad sense to smile, then feel like smiling; to act friendly and then become a friend; to give and then know what generosity is.

In fact, it may be just plain Christian to engage in Christian activity prior to or apart from good, pure motives. Maybe part of the failure of the church has been its inwardness, its tinkering with its soul to get tuned up for action. The old adages about not legislating morals, not forcing people to love each other, and so forth, have been true enough to perpetuate themselves but false enough to prevent attitudinal changes that *follow* rather than *precede* Christian conduct. New social contexts and civil issues, new patterns of thinking and living, of course, threaten and give rise to fear. Shall we wait until our heart is right to listen, read, participate, extend our hand? Is it possible that by acting like a Christian we may become one? God may move from hand to heart as well as from heart to hand. (Some cases in point come to mind.)

Method of sharing. Suppose the process described above matches somewhat the normal process of conceiving an idea, playing with it, wrestling with it, and bringing it to clarity; is there any reason why you could not repeat that process in the pulpit as your method of sharing? Read through it again and see if the method of personal preparation and the method of public proclamation are not, in terms of movement, much the same. It is too often the tragic fact about preaching that after the minister comes to a conclusion about a matter, it is that conclusion he announces, exhorts, illustrates, and repeats. Given the opportunity, the congregation could arrive at that conclusion, and it would be theirs.

And it would bear fruit.

Appendix B
Doxology
Romans 11:33–36

In this sermon I have sought to implement suggestions in the preceding essays, especially those dealing with movement, imagery, concrete life situations, and listener identification and participation. The reader is also asked to notice the attempt to make the form and spirit of the message congenial with the form and spirit of the text. Since the text is a doxology, a burst of praise in the midst of a theological discourse, so is the sermon. To have converted the text into a syllogism, or a polemic, or an exhortation, or a defense of a proposition would have been a literary, hermeneutical, aesthetic, and practical violation without excuse. Let doxologies be shared doxologically, narratives narratively, polemics polemically, poems poetically, and parables parabolically. In other words, biblical preaching ought to be biblical.

In the fall of the year, even after the days grow short and the air crisp, I still go out on the patio alone at the close of the day. It usually takes only a few minutes to knit up the raveled sleeve, quietly fold it, and put it away. But those few minutes are necessary; everyone needs a time and a place for such things.

But this particular evening was different. I sat there remembering, trying to understand the painful distance between the day as I planned it and the day as it had been. The growing darkness was seeping into mind and heart, and I was as the night. Looking back on it, I know now that it was this evening on which the Idea came to me. But frankly I was in no mood to entertain it.

It was not really a new Idea, but neither was it old. It was just an Idea. And it returned the next evening. I was relaxed enough to play with it a little while before it went away. The following evening I spent more time playing with the Idea and feeding it. Needless to say, I grew attached to the Idea before long, and then I had the fear that it belonged to one of the neighbors and that I would not be able to keep it. I went to each of the neighbors.

"Is this your Idea?"

"No, it isn't our Idea."

I claimed it for myself and exercised an owner's prerogative by giving it a name. I named it Doxology.

I took Doxology inside to our family supper table. Supper is family time, and conversation is usually reflection upon the day. If all are unusually quiet, I often ask, "What was the worst thing that happened today?"

John answers, "The school bell rang at 8:30."

"Well, what was the best thing that happened?"

"It rang again at 3:30."

Tongues are loosed and all of us— Laura, John, Nettie, and I— share our day. Supper is a good time and pleasant, and the whole family agreed Doxology belonged at our table.

The next day Doxology went with me downtown for some routine errands. But somehow they did not seem so routine. We laughed at a child losing a race with an ice cream cone, his busy tongue unable to stop the flow down to his elbow. We studied the face of a tramp staring in a jewelry store window and wondered if he were remembering better days or hoping for better days. We spoke to the banker, standing with thumbs in vest before a large plateglass window, grinning as one in possession of the keys of the kingdom. We were delighted by women shoppers clutching bundles and their skirts at blustery corners. It was good to have Doxology along.

But I had to make a stop at St. Mary's Hospital to see Betty. Betty was dying with cancer, and the gravity of my visit prompted me to leave Doxology in the car. Doxology insisted on going in and was not at all convinced by my reasons for considering it inappropriate to take Doxology into the room of a dying patient. I locked Doxology in the car.

Betty was awake and glad to see me. I awkwardly skirted the subject of death.

"It's all right," she said. "I know, and I have worked it through. God has blessed me with a wonderful family, good friends, and much happiness. I am grateful. I do not want to die, but I am not bitter." Before I left, it was she who had the prayer.

Back at the car, Doxology asked, "Should I have been there?"

"Yes. I'm sorry I did not understand."

Of course, Doxology went with the family on vacation. This summer we went to the beach down on the Gulf. What a good time! A swim before breakfast, a snooze in the afternoon sun, and a walk on the beach for shells in the evening. Doxology enjoyed watching the young people in dune buggies whiz by and spin sand over on the old man half-buried beside his wife, who turned herself in the sun like a chicken being barbecued. It was fun to walk out into the waves. These waves would start toward us, high, angry, and threatening, but as they drew near, they began to giggle and fall down. By the time they reached us, they had rolled over, we scratched their soft undersides, and they ran laughing back out to sea.

There is no question: Doxology belongs on a vacation.

Too soon it is school time again. I return to seminary classes, explaining all the while to Doxology that really Doxology is unnecessary, superfluous at seminary. After all, do we not spend the day every day talking about God, reading about God, writing about God? We do not need Doxology when we are heavily engaged in theology.

I was leading a group of students in a study of Paul's Letter to the Romans. The class soon discovered, however, that in this weightiest and most influential of all Paul's letters, the argument was often interrupted by Doxology. Early in the letter, in the midst of a discussion of the spiritual state of all those who live out their lives without Bible or knowledge of Christ, Paul insets a burst of praise to the "Creator who is blessed forever. Amen." After a very lengthy treatment of the tragic situation concerning the Jews, from whom came the Christ but who had not believed in Him, Paul breaks off his argument suddenly and begins to sing:

O the depth of the riches and wisdom and knowledge of God! How unsearchable are his judgments and how inscrutable his ways!

"For who has known the mind of the Lord? Or who has been
his counselor?"
"Or who has given a gift to him to receive a gift in return?"
For from him and through him and to him are all things. To
him be the glory forever. Amen.

Time and time again Paul breaks the line of thought with a
doxological reservation, as though suddenly reminding himself of
something. Why?

Probably because Paul is aware that the Doxology is most
appropriate to his task as a theologian. Theology begins with words
not *about* God but *to* God. People discern first what is sacred, and
from there move to what is true and right and good. Worship does
not interrupt theological study; theology grows out of worship.
And we do not attach chapel services to seminary life in order to
provide something extra; we worship because of what has already
been provided. A mother does not put a ribbon in her daughter's
hair to make her pretty, but because she is.

But more especially, the Doxology is appropriate for Paul's own
life, who he is. Who is Paul that he should write of the grand themes
of creation, the history of salvation, and redemption in Jesus Christ?
He is himself a creation of the very grace of which he speaks. He
offers himself as Exhibit A in evidence of the effective love of God.
Why not break into song now and then?

Nothing, in my opinion, could be more appropriate for any of
us, whoever or wherever or however. Whether we spend our time
at sticky cafe tables talking revolution or sit in calm indifference
on suburban patios, Doxology is not out of place.

While on sabbatical in Germany a few years ago, I was taken
by friends to a small hotel near Salzburg, Austria, where we had
dinner and heard a young woman sing. She was Julie Rayne, a
Judy Garland–type singer from London. Her songs were English,
German, and American, and so many of my old favorites were
included that I soon melted and ran down into the cracks of the
floor. During her performance, Miss Rayne sang one number of
unfamiliar tune but very familiar words:

I will lift up my eyes to the hills;
From whence comes my help?
My help comes from the Lord who made heaven and
earth.

What is going on here? If entertainers move into the field of religion, some of us will soon be out of work. I asked to speak with Miss Rayne and she consented. My question was, Why? Why, in the midst of popular songs, Psalm 121? Did it seem to her awkward and inappropriate? Her answer was that she had made a promise to God to include a song of praise in every performance. "If you knew what kind of person I was, and what I was doing," she said, "and what has happened since I gave my life to God, then you would know that Psalm 121 was the most appropriate song I sang."

Once in a while we have a seminarian who gives it up. Not suddenly but slowly; zeal cools, faith weakens, appetite for Christian enterprises disappears, the springs dry up, the soul is parched, and you can see it in eyes grown dull and flat. What happened? Did evil storm his citadel and take over? No. Did much study drive him into doubt? No. Did attractive alternatives to ministry turn his head? No. Nothing quite so dramatic. He simply made the fatal error of assuming that spending so much time talking *about* God was adequate substitute for talking *with* God. He lost his Doxology, and died.

Is there ever a time or place when it is inappropriate to say, "For from him and through him and to him are all things. To him be glory forever. Amen."?

It was from the class on Romans that I was called to the phone. My oldest brother had just died. Heart attack. When stunned and hurt, get real busy to avoid thought. Call the wife. Get the kids out of school. Arrange for a colleague to take my classes. Cancel a speaking engagement. And, oh yes, stop the milk, the paper, the mail; have someone feed the dog. Who can take my Sunday school class? Service the car. "I think I packed the clothes we need," the wife said as we threw luggage and our bodies into the car.

All night we drove, across two states, eyes pasted open against the windshield. Conversation was spasmodic, consisting of taking turns asking the same questions over and over. No one pretended to have answers. When we drew near the town and the house, I searched my mind for a word, a first word to the widow. He was my brother, but he was her husband. I was still searching when we pulled into the driveway. She came out to meet us, and as I opened the car door, still without that word, she broke the silence:

"I hope you brought Doxology."

Doxology?

No, I had not. I had not even thought of Doxology since the phone call.

But the truth is now clear: If we ever lose our Doxology, we might as well be dead.

"For from him and through him and to him are all things. To him be glory forever. Amen."

Appendix C
Asleep in the Storm
Mark 4: 34–41

I know that I read it, and it's in there, but it's hard for me to image Jesus asleep. In the gallery of images I have in my mind, his being asleep is not one of them. I can image him, I can picture him staying up all night in prayer; I picture him in Gethsemane praying until the early hours on the morning he was arrested—but not asleep. Now I know he had to sleep; everybody has to sleep. I don't have a spooky view of Jesus, that he never had to sleep. He had to sleep, just like I have to sleep, like you do, even on Sunday morning. But I think I don't want to picture him asleep. Sleeping is a very private thing. I don't think anybody should intrude on anyone else's sleep. The psychologists who study privacy and shame and embarrassment list among the intimate things that people do that are totally private—sleep. And I can understand it. We are vulnerable when we are asleep. We can come apart when we're asleep. Some people, when they're awake, hold themselves together quite well; when they go to sleep they kind of sprawl out all over the bed. They're awkward looking, unattractive. Some people drool, and I now and then hear reports of snoring. It's a very private thing, but it's a very complex thing. Sleeping is not just resting; sleeping is also a way of avoiding. It's a way of avoiding boredom. People who are bored, people who live in dull communities, people who have very dull jobs, according to the report, sleep many more hours than other people.

Sleep is a complex thing. It is for some people a way of avoiding responsibility. "Well, I was asleep. I was hoping it would be over when I woke up." Jonah was also a prophet in Israel, and he was also on a boat. He was also asleep, but he was running from responsibility. He got on a boat, bought a ticket to Tarsus, went down into the bottom of the boat, and went to sleep, hoping he could get away from God in his sleep. That's not what we have here. If there is a need to interpret the sleep of Jesus, I guess we could call it an act of total, complete trust. With a storm raging, dark at night on the Sea of Galilee, Jesus is in the back of the boat asleep. Usually if there is one in a group who is asleep, the others are given some calm by that, are put at ease by that: "It must not be as bad as we think if he's asleep. Why are we anxious?" As a mother during a thunderstorm will say to a child, "It's just clouds bumping together—don't worry about it, don't be afraid." Of course, if she says that while she's crawling under the bed, it doesn't really work. But one calm person in a group usually calms the group, and it may have here for a time. But when the waters start coming over into the boat, and they begin to bail the water, they rebuke Jesus: "Don't you care? We're dying here. Get a bucket, do something! It doesn't seem right that the leader should be asleep when we're feverishly fighting the storm and it looks like we're sinking."

I don't know what they expected, but he got up and rebuked the storm. "Hush!" The sea became glass, the winds stopped, and then he rebuked the disciples. "What's the matter with you fellows, have you no trust?" And they were even more scared, because if the storm is fierce, here is one stronger than the storm. And Mark says they were even more afraid.

I really, however, don't think it's necessary to interpret the sleep of Jesus. I think it makes more sense simply to say that he's totally exhausted. Mark uses an expression in this passage that is quite unusual. He said to his disciples, "Let's go over to the other side. And they took him"—listen to this—"in the boat, just as he was." What does it mean, "just as he was"? Whipped down, bedraggled, hungry, bent over already half asleep, in pain? What does it mean, "just as he was"? No time to clean up, freshen up, dress up, change clothes? Just as he was they took him. He's worn out. But that is unusual, isn't it? What's he been doing? He's been teaching. He's been preaching, he's been healing, he's been helping—aren't all these things exhilarating? "I could just do this all the time, helping, healing, teaching, preaching, giving, going, doing for people." Isn't that the most uplifting thing in the world? Why is he so whipped?

He isn't coming off a twelve-hour shift in a factory. He hasn't been digging potatoes all day. He's been helping. What is so exhausting about Christian work? What's so exhausting about ministry?

Well, this is a church of volunteers, you know as well as I do. My feeling is that part of the reason is that all Christian ministry, lay ministry, minister ministry, whatever kind—all of it grows out of idealism. There are people that God has placed in the world who feel keenly—*keenly*—the distance between what is and what ought to be. And they have this dream of making a major difference in the world, to cure all, fix all, help all, change all—everyone is going to be helped. It doesn't work that way. And the person falls into collapse and discouragement, and many times quits.

When I first was clear that God wanted me to be a minister, I had all these dreams when I said, "I give my life to Christian ministry." What does that mean, "I give my life"? I pictured myself swimming out there and rescuing someone drowning; jumping in front of a car and pulling a child back, even at the risk of my own life; standing before a gray wall with soldiers aiming their rifles— "Deny Jesus Christ and you can live." I refused, and the rifles fired, and I slumped, and there was weeping in the afternoon and flags at half-mast. It hasn't happened yet. I wanted to write God a check—my life—and now fifty years later I think the largest check I have written to God is 87 cents.

What is it to give your life? It's committee meetings, running to the hospital, talking with someone about their family, a funeral or a wedding now and then, studying for Sunday school class, going with a group to this or that. When do I get to give my life? And so it is a problem for people involved in Christian work that they have too low an opinion of the little bitty things, the checks for 39 cents and 87 cents. And they wonder, "When are we really going to get to do something big?" That's as big as it gets. And those of you—and I think this is most, if not all, of you—involved in doing good and right and Christian things for other people: Don't underestimate just a word, or a card, or a note, or a phone call.

On the plane coming back…I was there twice in Washington, for the celebration last week of the retirement of the organist at National City Church, and then I went back Thursday evening for a couple of days talking with some young people who are considering going into ministry. They gather every year to talk with one another and to have someone talk to them. On the way back I went to my assigned seat on the plane. It was 32D. The number of rows on this plane was 32. I was in the back row. I was between the engine and the toilet. I was against the wall. There were two seats on that side. There was stuff on the other side. It was a roaring, noisy mess back there. You get the picture? I'm at the end of it. The little kitchen thing is there, and the flight attendants are there doing their things, and we're getting ready to take off. I said, "I suppose you're going to do what you usually do." And she said, "What's that?" I said, "Start serving at the other end, at the front." And she said, "Well yes, we like to serve going toward people so they can see us coming and let their trays down and have in mind what they want to drink." And she said, "Why?" And I said, "I need a cup of coffee." And she leaned over and said, "I think I can give you a cup before I go down the aisle." I said, "Good!" There was a guy beside me but he was already hooked up to his laptop and earphones, and he was in another zone. I thought, *He doesn't know this; we'll do a little private business here.* So before they went down the aisle with the cart, she fixes me a cup and asks, "What do you want in it?" "Just a little milk, that's good." So she fixes me a cup of coffee, and this guy in another zone looks up and says, "I'll have the same." So she fixes him a cup. And the guy in front of me says, "I'll have orange juice." When is she going to stop? They went down the aisle serving backward. And when she got to the front and they came back, she said to me, "Look what you did!" I said, "I just wanted a cup of coffee." I asked her, "Were the people up there mad?" She said, "There was this one guy who was mad, but he was mad when he got on." All I said was, "Can I have a cup of coffee?" Now, if it can work on the plane with a cup of coffee, it'll work in your life. Just a kind word: Can I help you with that? I think I can fix that for you. Is it all right if I come Wednesday? I'd like to visit.

I had a phone call from a woman in Atlanta. I don't know her; I wouldn't know her if she came in. She said, "Last Sunday, we were there to ride the train and see the mountains, and we came to worship."

I said, "Good to have you; I want you to come back."

She said, "I stayed for your refreshment time and got to talking with a woman in your church, and it was so helpful to me, but I don't know her name and I want to write her a thank-you note. I wonder if you can help me?"

I said, "Well, would you describe her? Maybe I'll think of her."

She described you to a tee. I said, "Sure I know who that is!" I gave the name, and she said, "That's it!" I gave her the address, and somebody got a nice thank-you note from a lady in Atlanta when all you were doing was talking and having some nice refreshments. Just a little bit. A check for 41 cents. But they add up.

It is exhausting, especially when you get to that point when you think not everybody's participating. There are just a few of us doing the same things, you notice the same names coming up all the time. Where is everybody? When you begin to get that feeling— you know, like Elijah. Elijah, working himself to the ground as the prophet of Israel, looked around and he was by himself. Where is everybody? He looked up to God and said, "Why don't you kill me and end the whole story?" Do you have that feeling sometimes? Of course you do. Jesus did. He fed the five thousand, the disciples out counting the crowd counted five thousand. Did they have a crowd! But the problem with the disciples was that they didn't know the difference between a crowd and a congregation. Five thousand. They came the next morning for another meal, and Jesus said, "I have but one meal to offer you. My body and my blood. Will you walk with me the thorny way?" They drifted off, and out of five thousand he had twelve left. He said, "Are you fellows going to leave too?" And they said no.

But it does get kind of tiresome when you think you have a big bunch and you really don't. The one thing that really wears you out is when you try to work out your convictions and your service to Jesus Christ and you find opposition and tension and battle with your own people; people who should be encouraging and supporting and joining in are opposing. That's awful. Did you know there are some people who live the Christian life embattled? There was a time a few years ago, a generation ago, that different denominations fought and competed with one another. That's over. Every denomination is fighting itself. Every denomination I know is in a big battle. There's some group or another that wants to change everything, and it's really critical.

In Washington, these hundred and thirty brightest and best had been brought from California, New York, Georgia, everywhere, and I was privileged to talk to them about ministry, and after I finished my presentation, a young woman came up to me and said she was a university senior. There were several of them who wanted to know if I would give them some time after, and I said sure. So there were several of them who waited for me up front near the Chancel—this was at Wesley Theological Seminary in Washington—there were seventeen young women, all women; they were all university seniors from all over the country. They didn't belong to the same denomination. The seventeen represented three different denominations. Now, the spokesperson for the group said, "We never met till we came here. We don't all belong to the same church, but we have one thing in common. We believe that we have been called into the ministry. Our churches say we have not. Why? Because we're women. Do you have any advice?"

I talked with them. I said, "I would like to urge you to stay with the church that brought you up and taught you scriptures and led you to this point in your life. I would like to urge you to stay with that. It might change, it might change." One of them said, "I'm not the pioneering type. I have to have support and encouragement." "Well, maybe some of you can't, but whatever you do, do it with grace and generosity and appreciate the fact that somebody led you to this point and don't ever stomp on that or be ungrateful for that, even if you have to leave and go to some other fellowship." One of the women spoke up and said, "I am a twin. My twin is my brother, and we both feel that we've been called into the ministry, and my church said yes to him and no to me."

I said, "We shouldn't even be having this conversation." But they're going to make it. I can tell they're going to make it. I believe as surely as anything that God is stirring their hearts for something good and right and Christian for them to do. But it is hard. They'll get tired. I think probably a principal reason people get tired doing Christian work is that they're nervous in the presence of God and they won't go complain to God, so they just complain to one another. Why not just go to the boss? Make an appointment, go to God, and say, "Look, this is exactly how I feel about all this." God's pretty strong.

Bible characters did it. Moses made an appointment and went in to talk to God and said, "So this is how you work. Have a big exodus and we're free of Egypt and we're out here in the desert and we don't have any water and we don't have any food, and you say, 'You're on your own.' And all the other gods around here, all the pagan gods are saying, 'Boy, Israel's God doesn't know how to finish the job.' But if that's the way you want to do it...I just thought I'd bring it to your attention." And God said, "Moses, you have a point." God can handle that.

Sarah, Abraham's wife, came on her walker to keep her appointment with God. And when she finally got up there to God's desk, she said, "I'm nearly a hundred; I'm all bent over and worn out, wrinkled as a washboard, and now I get this word I'm having a baby. Do you hear me laughing? I'm laughing about this." And Jonah made an appointment. Jonah was sent to preach to Arabs.

He was as Jewish as you could get, and he was sent to preach to Arabs. He didn't want to, but he had to go. He did it, but he thought he would just bring the message of doom, and he started the countdown. But God had kindness and mercy; God's love and forgiveness overflowed. God forgave all those Arabs, and Jonah made an appointment. He walked in there and he said, "I didn't want to go in the first place. I knew you'd chicken out and forgive all those Arabs. We don't like Arabs. All this time we've been doing this, and you don't know the difference between Jews and Arabs? Arabs wear a different headdress. If you'll look carefully, they are different. I don't like you being kind to people I hate." And God listened. If you feel yourself sagging, not enough help, not enough respect for what you're doing for Christ, just make yourself an appointment. It'll be all right.

But I don't know anything like it, the service of Christ, as exhausting as it is. You probably read about it, the group of people whose leader said one Sunday evening, "I want us all to go on a trip." And they said, "Hey, yeah, let's wait and go this winter and go to Aspen and go skiing." "No, I had in mind a work trip." "Work?!" They said it as if he had said typhoid fever. Work? "Over in Eastern Kentucky, in Corbin County, people are very, very poor. Why don't we go up there for eight or ten days and do some work? Repair roofs, sagging porches, broken steps, put screens on windows that never had any screens." These kids were spoiled; none of them worked; their parents gave them everything. Finally, the upshot was that nine went with two adults, who knew what they were doing. They spent ten days up there. They slept in their bedrolls in churches. They ate in the kitchens of folks who gave them collard greens and field peas; they saw some worthless men lying around cursing their wives and drinking beer. They heard children crying in houses where there were twice as many children as there ought to be. They got a baptism into reality. They fixed the porch and fixed the roof and fixed the screens and fixed the steps. They came back home. All the bathing they'd done had been in a dishpan or in a creek; they used outhouses for toilets, these spoiled kids. They got back home and were lying around the parking lot waiting for their parents to pick them up, and one of the kids said, "This is the best tired I've ever been." You know what that is? "The best tired I've ever been."

Appendix D
Nothing Is Impossible with God
Luke 1:26–38

"For nothing will be impossible with God." That's the text, and it is a preacher's delight, because you don't have to go into who said what to whom and bring up Samuel or Saul or Moses or Paul or anybody. It's just one of those statements that's true without context. Nothing is impossible with God. You can put it in a bottle and toss it in the sea and have it wash up on a distant shore, and it's true. You can put it on a banner and have an airplane carry it across the sky, and it's true. You can write it on a slip of paper and put it under your pillow; it's true.

Nothing is impossible with God. It's like a proverb. It doesn't need who said it to whom or what or where; it's true. An ounce of prevention is worth a pound of cure. It's better to be safe than sorry. A bird in the hand is worth two in the bush. If your heart is bitter, sugar on your lips won't help. Some things are just true. This is just true. And you are therefore relieved of my having to go into a lot of Bible history in order to establish this. It's true. Now, I know it sounds as if it's from a fairy tale. What is the name of that book of children's stories? *Anything Is Possible*? Elves come in the night to fix things that are broken, and a beautiful princess touches things with her wand and all hurts are healed, and dirt turns to gold. All wishes come true, and animals talk to children, and nothing is impossible with God. It sounds like a fairy tale, but it isn't. It's from Holy Scripture. And it has been the anchor, the rock, the sustenance for people in extremely difficult circumstances. I heard this text once spoken through the bars of a jail to a prisoner who sat in there with his head in his hands crying, wondering what would happen to his wife and child. Nothing is impossible with God. You can write it with crayola in every orphanage; you can embroider it on a pillow in every nursing home. It is the truth. Nothing is impossible with God.

I remember the first time I heard it, was in Rhea County in the mountains of East Tennessee. A logger working in the hills pulling and snaking out the logs had been killed in an accident, leaving a widow and three small girls. He was already dead when I came to know her. She dressed those girls; they always looked clean; their hair was shiny; and they looked happy running down the road from their little cabin to catch the bus. They wore their little cotton dresses, always clean and pressed. Ruby got a check every month for $147. I said, "Ruby, you can't do it." And she said, "I'm going to be here when those kids go to school, and I'm going to be here when they get home, and I'll just pick up extra money where I can." She did washing and ironing. I said to her one day, "Now, Ruby, you can't do this on $147 a month: why don't you just come clean with me, I'm the minister. You're bootlegging." And she laughed and she said, "Nothing is impossible with God."

It was in Oklahoma, a place called Carrier, Oklahoma, that I heard this. I was a guest in a home. I was a guest in the pulpit, and they had invited me to lunch. I saw on the upright piano a picture of a young man wearing a uniform. "Your son?" "Yes." This was following the Korean War. I said, "He was in the war?" She said, "Yes." I said, "He's home now?" She said, "No." I said, "Was he killed?" She said, "No. He is missing in action." I said, "How many years?" She said, "It's been seven years, but we still have hope." And her husband, sitting at the end of the table, said, "We do not. We have no reason to hope anymore." And he threw his napkin down and walked out into the backyard. I said, "Should I go out there?" She said, "Oh, no. He hasn't given up. You see, nothing is impossible with God."

I don't know if you people know it, I don't know if I've told you, but I said that to myself a lot as we were starting this church. I hadn't planned on all this. As a minister of the Disciples of Christ I've always believed, of course, that people of all backgrounds, economic, social, educational, denominational, can come together in one faith in God as revealed in the forgiving love of Jesus Christ.

Whatever things we may believe, I've always believed that. And then you people came along and put that to the test.

Some of you are wastefully wealthy; some of you watch your pennies. Nothing is impossible with God. Some are so shy you stand around counting your shoelaces. Others come bursting into a room and get the name of everybody they've never met before. Some sit outside waiting for someone they know so they can come in together, they are so shy. Others are happy in the presence of strangers. We can't make a church out of that, can we? Nothing is impossible with God.

And how are we going to get any young people interested? Young people like to be where there are a lot of folks; they like to be where there are 150 kids knocking and talking. How can you have a church where there are just a few? They don't like to come where there are just a few. They have a kind of herd instinct, and we don't have a herd.

When we were in West Tennessee for Miss Auttie's funeral, the great-grandchildren were there sitting around on the furniture wishing they were somewhere else, I said to one of them, "Boy, it got cold last night." He said, "Yeah." I said, "I don't know how cold it got, but Miss Auttie has a thermometer out on the porch." And he went out to read the thermometer, and some of the others went, and then six of them went out there to read the thermometer. I said to myself, *We don't even have six*. But nothing is imposssible with God.

We have people who don't read the Bible, and we have people here who are Bible teachers. Nothing is impossible with God. We have some people who show up every time we have a Bible study or worship. They show up because they want to build their reserve and make deposits on their faith so that when the crisis comes, they can write a check and be sustained. We have others that don't really worry about that. I'll handle whatever comes...They don't know that they can't.

When I was a kid, there was a little house on the empty farm next to ours. A family moved in, didn't stay long. It was wintertime, there was a little stove, a woodburning stove, and the man would go outside to the back of the house and pull boards off to burn in the stove. And as it got colder, he pulled off more boards. And it got colder. He pulled off more boards. And it got colder. And he pulled off more boards, and it really got cold, and so he and his wife left, and they cursed the stove and they cursed the house. And there was an ax and a chopping block and a tree and another tree and a forest available, and he burned up his own house to warm his own house. And I thought about how many people there are who think they have their own resources, their own strength, their own power to handle it when the phone rings, the letter comes, and the crisis is too big. I thought, *I don't know*. And the text came back, Nothing is impossible with God. That's where we started. And here we are. But you know me well enough to know that whatever the text is, I cannot pull it out of the context; it is a part of Holy Scripture, and we need to know who said it to whom. Nothing is impossible with God—it is twice in the Bible, I guess you know. It appears once in the Old Testament and once in the New Testament. The circumstances are very similar, but different. In the Old Testament it's in Genesis 18. An old couple named Abraham and Sarah have no children, absolutely none, no kids, and they're old. And a messenger of God comes to their tent one day and says, "You're going to have children. You'll conceive and have a son, and from him will come a nation, and that nation will bless the world." And Sarah laughed and said, "You've got to be kidding!" And she had the son, and she named him laughter, *Isaac*, because it seemed so funny to her.

And from Isaac came the nation we call Israel, and Israel, in spite of being enslaved, persecuted, murdered, ostracized, made fun of, unwelcome, has given the world the basis for a moral and ethical society. You should love the Lord your God with all your mind and heart and soul and strength, and your neighbor as yourself. That's the foundation. You shall not kill; you shall not bear false witness against a neighbor; you shall not covet what your neighbor has. You shall not murder; you shall honor your marriage vows. Have no other God before me, have no idols, and remember the Sabbath day and keep it holy. You need your rest. God rested. And in those commandments we have the basis for the whole Western world's life together. And it started when a messenger said to an old couple, "You're going to have a baby. And the world will be blessed." That's in Genesis 18.

In Luke 1 it is almost the same, but different. To Sarah and to Abraham the messenger said, Nothing is impossible to God. To Mary, a teenage girl in a little town in northern Israel, unmarried— she had been promised by her family to a carpenter who lived there in Nazareth by the name of Joseph, but they were not yet married— the messenger said, "You're going to have a child." "But I don't have a husband!" "You're going to have a child, and he will bless the world." And she did. And in spite of the fact that he was mistreated, abandoned, made fun of, mocked, beaten, whipped, and executed, wherever he goes, people's hearts are lifted. They become kind and generous. People who remember Jesus will repair their neighbor's house when their own roof leaks. They'll empty their pockets for other people's children. "Is there any way I can help?" They'll love even their enemies. They will turn the other cheek. They'll go the second mile. And all because a messenger said, "You're going to have a child and you'll name him Jesus." And Mary said, "I don't get it." And the angel said, "Nothing—nothing—is impossible with God."

Now folks, I hope we've all learned our lesson by now. It's been two thousand years. If God can give a child to an old couple in a tent in Saudi Arabia and change the world; if God can give a baby to a teenage girl in northern Israel and change the world, why should you ever, why should I ever, give up hope, doubt, wonder, despair, shrug my shoulders? I think, I think, *I think* I have learned my lesson: Nothing is impossible with God.

Write that over the door at your house. Write that on your mind. Write that across your heart. It will come in handy before we meet again. Nothing, nothing is impossible with God.

Amen.

Appendix E
And They Said Nothing to Anyone
Mark 16:8

The earliest account, which was just read, of Easter morning—Mark 16—begins without any real surprises. Three women, whose names we know—Salome, Mary, called the Magdalene, and Mary the mother of James—went to the cemetery after the funeral. This is not unusual. This has been a practice in my family after the loss of a member of the family; some of us go to the cemetery again later. There may be a card still left in flowers and we need to send a thank-you note; there may be some flowers, still fresh enough that we may need to take to a church or a nursing home. And it's a quiet time because the crowd is gone. It's not unusual to go to the cemetery after the funeral. These three women went because it was up to them to care for the body. Nobody did that officially. The climate was such, the practices such, and in this case with such a hasty burial, that they had work left to do, to put spices on the corpse. No surprise. But then wave after wave of surprises begin. The grave is open. They're shocked and immediately disturbed. Then a young man in dazzling white is standing there, and they say, "Jesus?" "No, he's not here, he has risen just as he said. But he left a message for you; he wants you to go and tell his disciples and Peter that 'I will go before them into Galilee. I will meet them there. They will see me.'" It's too much for the women. Instead of going with the commission that Christ has given them, to go and tell the disciples, they run the other way. They are traumatized, they're amazed, they're shocked, they're afraid, and they are completely silent. The language of the New Testament, the Greek language, allows, as most languages do, that you can break the rules of grammar sometimes in order to emphasize a point. And literally what is said of the women is this: They did not say nothing to nobody. In other words, totally silent.

Now, since the second century the church has not liked the ending of Mark. This is no way to run a resurrection! Having women quiet, not saying anything, and scared and running. And so starting in the second century scribes began to add to the gospel of Mark. And if you look in your Bible, most of you will find an alternate ending, a short ending, a mixed ending, taking pieces of the other gospels and adding them to Mark so that it will have an appearance of Christ, triumphant resurrection morning, belief of the disciples, and a lot of hallelujah. My old teacher in seminary said that the reason Mark ends the way it does is that the end of it apparently got frayed or damaged or destroyed, and we don't know exactly how it ended. I'm comfortable with the way it ended. The women were totally silent. I can understand that. You have to give them some time to doubt this. The men had time to doubt it. All the gospels say that some of the twelve disciples doubted it. Matthew says, "They worshiped him; but some doubted." Luke says, "While in their joy they were disbelieving." Feel the mixture there of believing and not believing? And John says Simon Peter said, "Well I'm going fishing." And Thomas, one of the twelve, said, "Well, I won't believe it till I touch him." Why not let the women have time to question the truth of it? Or it could be that they just don't need any more news. I don't care how good it is, you just reach a saturation point of not needing any more news. And they are in a position to need nothing else. Jesus is dead and buried. They've cleaned out his closet; they've given away what few things he had. They have washed and returned the dishes to those who brought food. They've written the thank-you notes. The dog has been returned from the vet. The guests are gone. Four loads of laundry have been done. And now comes the routine, the blessed, joyous routine, of life as it was. You can complain all you want about routine; there is nothing so composing, so giving of composure, as routine. Let's get back to our routine. They don't need any news, however good it is. They can't hold it. But the text says they were afraid. It doesn't say of whom; maybe the authorities. Very likely the authorities. In order to keep law and order, they killed Jesus. He's a rabble-rouser, got a lot of people stirred up, created a lot of dissension, huddles of people planning and plotting on street corners. We have to get rid of him in the name of law and order! And so they did.

Now let's suppose we go out and say Jesus is alive again. You know what they're going to do? They're going to start with us. And they can squash us like bugs. Because how many do we have? Luke says, after all Jesus' ministry, he had 120 believers. Less than the membership of this one congregation. If Josephus was right and there were more than 2 million pilgrims in Jerusalem for the Passover, what would this little group of three women do in that kind of throng? They would be run over. What are you going to do?

Roman historians say that at the end of the first century the empire had a population of about 70 million. And they estimate that there were maybe as many as forty thousand Christians. Think of it. In a town of seven thousand people, four Christians. This means that in Gilmer and Fannin counties together after a hundred years there would be what? Seventeen? Most of us don't know what minority is. Think about it. Are they now going to get out the word that this Jesus you killed is alive again? Maybe that's what it is when he says they were scared. It could have been that they were simply unable to talk. Fear does that to you. Those of you who have been in your first play or led your first program or read scripture in public know what the fear is. Fear of mispronouncing, fear of choking up, fear of losing your voice, fear of falling down, fear of everything. It's hard to talk when you are deeply affected. We can chat about the weather and everything under the sun, but let someone bring up a sacred subject, and most of us get as quiet as these women, and we don't say nothing to nobody. The most common thing said to me in this church, which is run by volunteers, people who are good people— they cut down trees, mow the grass, wash the windows, serve, fix the table, decorate, bring flowers— but the one thing I hear most is this: "Don't ask me to say anything." I'll do anything, but don't ask me to say anything. I'll climb up and change the lightbulb, but don't ask me to say anything. Why is it that we can just chatter like magpies, but mention Jesus Christ and it's "Don't ask me to say anything"? I hear an expression a lot these days—it's not enough to talk the talk, you've got to walk the walk. Well, that's nice. The trouble with it is, it's backwards. It's not enough to walk the walk. You've got to talk the talk. Because the most difficult and most effective and most profound thing you'll ever do for Jesus Christ is to say something. And when I ask for talkers, no one comes. If I say, "Let's redo the building," everybody comes. This is no criticism of anyone, but an honest recognition that the fundamental human sacrament is to say something important. And that's hard to do.

Now Nettie and I and some other friends were talking recently with a man whose wife is very ill; she has been for many years. And one in the group asked him as we were leaving, "Is there anything we can do?" And he said, "Pray for her." Now when he said that, it was not only an indication of how sick she is, but it was a milestone in that man's life. I have known him for fifteen years and I had never heard him say anything so deep as that. It came from way down here. He can talk so freely of golf and the Braves and the Hawks and the weather and politics and the stock market. But I had never heard him say, "Pray for her."

These women couldn't talk. It might have been that they were afraid of the response. You take any good Christian witnesses and run them around a few times through the beauty parlors and the barber shops, through Wal-Mart and into the restaurants and the post office and one of those cafes where men sit all day drinking their coffee, and say "Jesus Christ is risen", and see what happens. Did you hear what those women said? They said he was risen! You're kidding? No! That sounds like a bunch of women who don't have enough to do. My goodness. Well, how do you explain it? They went to the wrong tomb, they were confused, it was early in the morning, they say it was about dark. They just got confused and went to the wrong tomb.

How do you explain it? Well, they moved the body; he was buried in someone else's tomb. They didn't have time, it was nearly sundown, they had to get him off the cross and get him buried. They just buried him nearby. They were going to move him later to a permanent place. What's the deal?

How do you explain it? They stole the body. Some of his followers stole his body and then started spreading this story about how he's raised from the dead, he's raised from the dead. It's the oldest trick in the world. Now you see it, now you don't.

How do you explain it? Well, I never believed he was dead in the first place. Really? Now, you just think about it. He was on the cross from, what, nine in the morning to a little after three? Listen, I've seen crucifixions, I've seen fellows hanging up there for three and four days, just think about it—they take him down from up there around three o'clock, and he hasn't been up there even a day? Half a day? Now you just think about it. That's premature burial. He came around. That's the way I look at it.

I just hate for our Christian witness to just get all messed up, to go through the rumor mills, and it comes back, and you don't know anything about it.

Now I want to say to you people as plain as I can on this Easter day that "Jesus Christ is risen from the dead" is a Christian witness. A church witness. It is something believers say. It's not a public statement. The risen never made an appearance in public. The only ones who saw him were his followers. No public appearances. If I had been running it, I would have had him go around to stores, go back into Pilate's hall and say, "Hey Pontius, you want to give it another shot?" That's the way I would have run it. And for people who doubted, agnostics and atheists and those sorts, I'd have had Jesus appear and just scare them to death. But that just shows you how small I am. If you read the New Testament, nobody saw him except his followers. If the world is going to believe it, they're going to believe it because you believe it and you testify to it, that's it. Luke said it just as plain as day. He said, "The life of Jesus you all know, it's a matter of public record. The death of Jesus is also a matter of public record. The resurrection of Jesus? Of that we're witnesses." Do you see? We cannot expect the public, the culture, society in general to sustain the real meaning of Easter. It is a Christian word. A Christian commitment. A Christian belief. One of the darkest, darkest times in the history of the world came when a man stood up in front of his country, his government, and said, "We can't expect the churches and the Christian families to carry the whole weight of ridding the world of atheism and communism. We have to put the power of government behind it." And so Adolf Hitler persuaded the people to put the power of government behind the battle to rid the world of atheism and communism. And he said, "God is with us."

We can neither be seduced nor intimidated by institutions or culture at large. It is a Christian message. Jesus Christ is raised. If the message of Easter is lost, and dwindles down and peters out, it becomes nothing more than colored eggs and rabbits, breaks from school, trips to the beach, spring holiday. If it becomes only that, it's not the schools' fault. It's not the government's fault. It's not society's fault. It's the church's fault. Because it is the church's message. And everybody's yelling about how the schools ought to do this and the government ought to pass a law about that—phooey on that! It is the church's message. It is for the church to say.

Now what are we going to say? We can't be like those who didn't say nothing to nobody. This is what I say: Our God is a God who gives life to the dead. It's been that way since creation. He brought into being what didn't exist and out of chaos formed the world. That's the way God is. God gives life to the dead. Or Abraham and Sarah, so old they couldn't have kids, they were over a hundred. And yet they believed God gives life to the dead, and even though both were so old they were dead as far as procreation was concerned, they had a child and named him *laughter*, Isaac. Jesus was dead. He was dead. You ask his friends, he's dead; you ask his mother, he's dead; and yet we believe that God gives life to the dead. You and I, dead in our trespasses and sins, God has made alive. Do you believe that? Can you think of a way of saying that? Can we say that to somebody? It's not enough to walk the walk, we have to talk the talk. We cannot be a church that runs from the empty tomb, silent. Amen.

Notes

CHAPTER 1: The Pulpit in the Shadows

[1]Joseph Sittler, *The Anguish of Preaching* (Philadelphia: Fortress Press, 1966), pp. 7, 12.

[2]Dr. John R. Killinger, Jr., "Preaching in a Post-Christian Age" (address given at Vanderbilt University, Nashville, November 3, 1964).

[3]Gerhard Ebeling, *God and Word*, trans. James W. Leitch (Philadelphia: Fortress Press, 1967), p. 8.

[4]Dallas M. High, *Language, Persons and Belief* (New York: Oxford Univ. Press, 1967), p. 137.

[5]Max Picard, *The World of Silence*, trans. Stanley Godman (Chicago: Henry Regnery, 1952), pp. 26–27.

[6]Ebeling, *God and Word*, p. 7.

[7]High, pp. 8–9.

[8]Ernst Cassirer, *Language and Myth*, trans. Susanne K. Langer (New York: Dover, 1946), p. 7.

[9]Kendrick Grobel, "Revelation and Resurrection," in *New Frontiers of Theology*, ed. James M. Robinson and John B. Cobb, Jr. (New York: Harpers, 1967), 3:158.

[10]Walter J. Ong, *The Presence of the Word* (New Haven: Yale Univ. Press, 1967), pp. 15–16.

[11]Ibid., p. 54. Ong has persuasively developed the idea of the change in the modern human's sensorium.

[12]Robert W. Funk, *Language, Hermeneutic, and Word of God* (New York: Harpers, 1966), p. 9.

[13]Thomas Wieser, "Evangelism and the 'Death of God'," *The Ecumenical Review* 20, no. 2 (1968): p. 140.

[14]Gerhard Ebeling, *Theology and Proclamation*, trans. John Riches (Philadelphia: Fortress Press, 1966), p. 15.

[15]Ibid., p. 18.

[16]Sittler, p. 50.

[17]Reuel Howe, *Partners in Preaching* (New York: Seabury Press, 1967), p. 35.

[18]James B. Conant, *Two Modes of Thought* (New York: Trident Press, 1964). Dr. Conant's point has been applied to the church by Locke Bowman, Jr., *Straight Talk About Teaching in Today's Church* (Philadelphia: Westminster Press, 1967).

[19]Howe, p. 47.

[20]Franz Kafka, *Parables and Paradoxes* (New York: Schocken Books, 1961), p. 93.

[21]Howe, p. 52.

CHAPTER 2: The Pulpit in the Spotlight

[1]Ong, pp. 292–93.

[2]Iris Murdoch, *Sartre* (New Haven: Yale Univ. Press, 1953), p. 27.

[3]Ong, p. 22.

[4]Funk, p. 12.

[5]Ong, p. 88.

[6]Gerhard Ebeling, *The Nature of Faith*, trans. R. G. Smith (Philadelphia: Muhlenberg Press, 1961), p. 186.

[7]Marshall McLuhan, *Understanding Media* (New York: McGraw Hill, 1964), pp. 22–23.

[8]Clemens E. Benda, "Language, Consciousness and Problems of Existential Analysis," *American Journal of Psychotherapy* 14, no. 2 (April, 1960), quoted by Amos Wilder, *The Language of the Gospel* (Cambridge: Harvard Univ. Press, 1970), p. 19.

[9]Ong, pp. 200–299.

[10]For pursuit of these directions, consult *The Journal of Pastoral Care, Pastoral Psychology*, and Edgar N. Jackson, *A Psychology for Preaching* (Great Neck, N. Y.: Channel Press, 1961).

[11]Albert H. van den Heuvel, *The Humiliation of the Church* (Philadelphia: Westminster Press, 1966), p. 71.

[12]Ong, pp. 138–44.

[13]Alfred North Whitehead, *Modes of Thought* (New York: Capricorn Books, 1938), pp. 45–57.

[14]Alfred North Whitehead, *Religion in the Making* (New York: Macmillan, 1926), p. 131.

[15]W. D. Hudson, *Ludwig Wittgenstein: The Bearing of His Philosophy upon Religious Belief* (Richmond, Va.: John Knox Press, 1968), pp. 46–47.

[16]Sam Keen, *Gabriel Marcel* (Richmond, Va.: John Knox Press, 1967), p. 47.

[17]Georges Gusdorf, *Speaking*, trans. Paul T. Brockelman (Evanston, Ill.: Northwestern Univ. Press, 1965), pp. 119–27.

[18]J. L. Austin, *Philosophical Papers* (Oxford: Clarendon Press, 1961), pp. 222–24. Also, *How to Do Things with Words*, ed. J. 0. Urmson (New York: Oxford Univ. Press, 1965).

[19]Cassirer, Gusdorf, and Austin, all referred to earlier, give such surveys.

[20]Gerhard von Rad, *Old Testament Theology*, trans. D. M. G. Stalker (New York: Harpers, 1965), 2:86.

[21]Cf. esp. Wisdom of Solomon, chaps. 6—9.

[22]Martin Heidegger, *Existence and Being*, trans. Stefan Schimanski (Chicago: Henry Regnery, 1949), p. 270.

[23]Ibid,. p. 277.

[24]W. M. Urban, *Language and Reality* (London: Allen and Unwin, 1939), p. 49.

[25]Gerhard Ebeling, *Word and Faith*, trans. James W. Leitch (Philadelphia: Fortress Press, 1963), p. 329.

[26]Especially by Ebeling and Funk, and by Ernst Fuchs of the University of Marburg.

[27]Funk, p. 11.

[28]Ibid, p. 7.

[29]Ong, pp. 12–13.

[30]Amos Wilder, *The Language of the Gospel* (Cambridge/Harvard Univ. Press, 1970), p. 24; cf. pp. 18–24.

[31]Ibid., p. 22.

[32]Ibid., p. 11.

[33]Funk.

[34]Cf. the bibliography in Domenico Grazzo, *Proclaiming God's Message* (South Bend, Ind.: University of Notre Dame Press, 1965).

CHAPTER 3: Inductive Movement in Preaching

[1]But this is changing. Werner Jetter, Professor of Preaching at Tübingen, has written *(Wem predigen wir?* [Stuttgart: Calwer Verlag, 1964], p. 46) to the effect that

the preacher must treat his hearers as mature men of the world and learn to hear his own words with their ears. Manfred Mezger, *Verkündigung heute* (Hamburg: FurcheVerlag, 1966), writes in the same vein.

[2]Bruno Dreher, *Biblische Predigten* (Stuttgart: Verlag Katholisches Bibelwerk, 1968), pp. 97ff.

[3]Dwight E. Stevenson, *In the Biblical Preacher's Workshop* (Nashville: Abingdon Press, 1967), pp. 200–201, distinguishes deductive and inductive by whether the text comes first or last. By induction, I mean the entire movement of the sermon, including use of the text, which may be approached early in the sermon.

[4]Locke Bowman, Jr., *Straight Talk about Teaching in Today's Church* (Philadelphia: Westminster Press, 1967), pp. 33ff.

[5]Elton Abernathy, *The Advocate* (New York: David McKay Co., 1964), p. 64.

[6]Funk, pp. 69–70, 156.

[7]William F. Lynch, *Images of Hope* (New York: The New American Library, 1965), p. 169.

[8]Rudolf Bultmann, "Points of Contact and Conflict," in *Essays: Philosophical and Theological*, trans. James Grieg (New York: Macmillan, 1955), pp. 133–50. An excellent discussion of this problem is to be found in James E. Sellers, *The Outsider and the Word of God* (Nashville: Abingdon Press, 1961).

[9]Ebeling, *Word and Faith*, p. 320.

[10]C. H. Dodd, *The Parables of the Kingdom* (New York: Charles Scribner's Sons, 1961), p. 5.

[11]Erik Routley, *Into a Far Country* (London: Independent Press, 1962), pp. 20ff.

[12]Carl Michalson, "Theology as Ontology and as History," in *New Frontiers in Theology*, ed. James M. Robinson and John B. Cobb, Jr. (New York: Harpers, 1963), 1:143–51.

[13]Gustaf Wingren, *Die Predigt*, 2d ed. (Göttingen: Vandenhoeck und Ruprecht, 1959), pp. 31–32.

[14]Manfred Mezger, *Verkündigung heute* (Hamburg: FurcheVerlag, 1966), p. 38.

[15]Nathaniel Micklem, *The Labyrinth Revisited* (London: Oxford Univ. Press, 1960), p. 31.

[16]Dietrich Bonhoeffer, *No Rusty Swords: Letters, Lectures and Notes 1928–36*, from *The Collected Works of Dietrich Bonhoeffer*, ed. Edwin H. Robertson, trans. Edwin H. Robertson and John Bowden, vol. 1 (New York: Harper and Row, 1965), pp. 161–62.

CHAPTER 4: Inductive Preaching and the Imagination

[1]John Macquarrie, *Martin Heidegger* (Richmond, Va.: John Knox Press, 1968), p. 48.

[2]Alfred North Whitehead, *Process and Reality* (New York: Macmillan, 1929), p. 7.

[3]Ong, p. 51.

[4]Lynch.

[5]Marshall McLuhan and Quentin Fiore, *The Medium is the Massage* (New York: Random House, 1967), p. 93.

[6]Ebeling, *The Nature of Faith*, p. 190.

[7]William F. Lynch, *Christ and Apollo* (New York: The New American Library, 1960), p. 77.

[8]Dietrich Bonhoeffer, *Letters and Papers from Prison*, rev. ed., trans. R. Fuller, (New York: Macmillan, 1967), p. 161.

CHAPTER 5: Inductive Movement and the Unity of the Sermon

[1]Igor Stravinsky, *Poetics of Music in the Form of Six Lessons* (Cambridge: Harvard Univ. Press, 1970), p. 87.

[2]Howe, p. 59.

[3]See the perceptive discussion of this problem in Sittler, pp. 1–11.

[4]van den Heuvel, p. 66.

[5]Ebeling, *Word and Faith*, p. 325.

[6]James M. Robinson, "Hermeneutic since Barth," in *New Frontiers in Theology*, ed. James M. Robinson and John B. Cobb, Jr. (New York: Harpers, 1964), 2:177.

[7]Sittler, pp. 20ff.

[8]Amos Wilder, "The Word as Address and the Word as Meaning," in *New Frontiers in Theology*, ed. James M. Robinson and John B. Cobb, Jr. (New York: Harpers, 1964), 2:198–218.

[9]C. H. Dodd, *The Apostolic Preaching and Its Development* (London: Hodder and Stoughton, Ltd., 1936).

[10]For an excellent discussion of the Dodd/Bultmann tension, cf. William R. Baird, "What is the Kerygma?" *Journal of Biblical Literature* 76 (1957): pp. 181–91.

CHAPTER 6: Inductive Movement and the Text

[1]Ebeling, *Theology and Proclamation*, p. 14.

[2]Joachim Jeremias, *The Parables of Jesus*, 6th ed., trans. S. H. Hooke (New York: Scribner's, 1962), pp. 42–48.

[3]Willi Marxsen, "Exegese und Verkundigung," *Theologische Existenz Heute*, neue Folge, 59 (1957): 113.

[4]Manfred Mezger, "Preparation for Preaching," trans. Robert Kraft, in *Translating Theology into the Modern Age: Journal for Theology and the Church* (New York: Harpers, 1965), 2:165.

[5]Ebeling, *Word and Faith*, p. 329.

[6]Marxsen, p. 50.

[7]Mezger, "Preparation for Preaching," p. 174.

[8]The view of J. J. von Allmen, *Preaching and Congregation*, trans. B. L. Nicholas (London: Lutterworth Press, 1962), p. 27.

[9]Bonhoeffer, *Letters and Papers*, pp. 2–4.

[10]Mezger, "Preparation for Preaching," p. 176.

[11]Wilder, "The Word as Address," pp. 20–56.

[12]C. F. Sleeper, "Language and Ethics in Biblical Interpretation," *The Journal of Religion* 48, no. 3 (1968), pp. 288–310.

[13]Marxsen, p. 56.

[14]Robert Funk, "The Hermeneutical Problem and Historical Criticism," in *New Frontiers in Theology*, ed. James M. Robinson and John B. Cobb, Jr. (New York: Harpers, 1964), 2:167–80.

[15]Ernst Fuchs, "Must One Believe in Jesus if He Wants to Believe in God?" *Journal for Theology and the Church* 1 (1964):154.

[16]Ebeling, *Word and Faith*, pp. 312–13.

[17]Karl Barth, *Prayer and Preaching* (London: SCM Press, 1964), p. 71.

CHAPTER 7: Inductive Movement and Structure

[1]Micklem, p. 1.

[2]For example, cf. the discussion of the parable of the marriage feast (Luke 14; Matt. 22) in Eta Linnemann, *Jesus of the Parables*, trans. John Sturdy (New York: Harpers, 1966), pp. 88–96.

[3]Edgar Allan Poe, "Philosophy of Composition," in *The Complete Poetical Works of Edgar Allan Poe*, ed. John Ingram (n.p.: A. L. Burt Co., n.d.), pp. 255–72.

[4]Thomas de Quincey, "On Murder," *De Quincey's Works* (New York: Houghton, 1882), 6:573.

[5]The familiar insistence of Hermann Diem that the sermon stay in the text, moving as it moves. *Warum Textpredigt?* (Müinchen: Chr. Kaiser Verlag, 1939), pp. 197–221.

[6]Wilder, *The Language of the Gospel*.

[7]Ibid., p. 13.

[8]As Mezger properly characterizes a sermon in "Preparation for Preaching," p. 177.

[9]Karl Barth's theological objections to introductions cannot be accepted as valid in view of the modern speaker/hearer relationship. Cf. *Prayer and Preaching*, pp. 110–11.